FREEDOM OF SPEECH

Other books in this series:

The Bill of Rights

FREEDOM
OF SPEECH

Edited by William Dudley

Bruce Glassman, *Vice President*
Bonnie Szumski, *Publisher*
Helen Cothran, *Managing Editor*
Scott Barbour, *Series Editor*

GREENHAVEN PRESS
An imprint of Thomson Gale, a part of The Thomson Corporation

THOMSON
™
GALE

Detroit • New York • San Francisco • San Diego • New Haven, Conn.
Waterville, Maine • London • Munich

THOMSON

GALE

LIBRARY OF CONGRESS CATALOGING-IN-PUBLICATION DATA

Freedom of speech / William Dudley, book editor.
    p. cm. — (The Bill of Rights)
Includes bibliographical references and index.
ISBN 0-7377-1929-X (lib. : alk. paper)
    1. Freedom of speech—United States—History. I. Dudley, William, 1964– .
II. Bill of Rights (San Diego, Calif.)

KF4772.A75F74 2005
342.7308'53—dc2
    2004054149

CONTENTS

Chapter 2: Balancing Free Speech, Community Order, and National Security

Chapter 3: Obscenity and Freedom of Expression

the Supreme Court attempted once again to define obscenity and place it outside the bounds of First Amendment protection.

Chapter 4: Recent and Ongoing Controversies over Free Speech and the First Amendment

"I cannot agree with those who think of the Bill of Rights as an 18th Century straightjacket, unsuited for this age. . . . The evils it guards against are not only old, they are with us now, they exist today."

—Hugo Black, associate justice of the
U.S. Supreme Court, 1937–1971

The Bill of Rights codifies the freedoms most essential to American democracy. Freedom of speech, freedom of religion, the right to bear arms, the right to a trial by a jury of one's peers, the right to be free from cruel and unusual punishment—these are just a few of the liberties that the Founding Fathers thought it necessary to spell out in the first ten amendments to the U.S. Constitution.

While the document itself is quite short (consisting of fewer than five hundred words), and while the liberties it protects often seem straightforward, the Bill of Rights has been a source of debate ever since its creation. Throughout American history, the rights the document protects have been tested and reinterpreted. Again and again, individuals perceiving violations of their rights have sought redress in the courts. The courts in turn have struggled to decipher the original intent of the founders as well as the need to accommodate changing societal norms and values.

The ultimate responsibility for addressing these claims has fallen to the U.S. Supreme Court. As the highest court in the nation, it is the Supreme Court's role to interpret the Constitution. The Court has considered numerous cases in which people have accused government of impinging on their rights. In the process, the Court has established a body of case law and precedents that have, in a sense, defined the Bill of Rights. In doing so, the Court has often reversed itself and introduced new ideas and approaches that have altered the legal meaning of the rights contained in the Bill of Rights. As a general rule, the Court has erred on the side of caution, upholding and expanding the rights of individuals rather than restricting them.

An example of this trend is the definition of cruel and unusual punishment. The Eighth Amendment specifically states, "Excessive bail shall not be required, nor excessive fines imposed, nor cruel and unusual punishments inflicted." However, over the years the Court has had to grapple with defining what constitutes "cruel and unusual punishment." In colonial America, punishments for crimes included branding, the lopping off of ears, and whipping. Indeed, these punishments were considered lawful at the time the Bill of Rights was written. Obviously, none of these punishments are legal today. In order to justify outlawing certain types of punishment that are deemed repugnant by the majority of citizens, the Court has ruled that it must consider the prevailing opinion of the masses when making such decisions. In overturning the punishment of a man stripped of his citizenship, the Court stated in 1958 that it must rely on society's "evolving standards of decency" when determining what constitutes cruel and unusual punishment. Thus the definition of cruel and unusual is not frozen to include only the types of punishment that were illegal at the time of the framing of the Bill of Rights; specific modes of punishment can be rejected as society deems them unjust.

Another way that the Courts have interpreted the Bill of Rights to expand individual liberties is through the process of "incorporation." Prior to the passage of the Fourteenth Amendment, the Bill of Rights was thought to prevent only the federal government from infringing on the rights listed in the document. However, the Fourteenth Amendment, which was passed in the wake of the Civil War, includes the words, ". . . nor shall any state deprive any person of life, liberty, or property, without due process of law; nor deny to any person within its jurisdiction the equal protection of the laws." Citing this passage, the Court has ruled that many of the liberties contained in the Bill of Rights apply to state and local governments as well as the federal government. This process of incorporation laid the legal foundation for the civil rights movement—most specifically the 1954 *Brown v. Board of Education* ruling that put an end to legalized segregation.

As these examples reveal, the Bill of Rights is not static. It truly is a living document that is constantly being reinterpreted and redefined. The Bill of Rights series captures this vital aspect of one of America's most cherished founding texts. Each volume in the series focuses on one particular right protected in the Bill of Rights. Through the use of primary and secondary sources, the right's evolution is traced from colonial times to the present. Primary sources include landmark Supreme Court rulings, speeches by prominent experts, and editorials. Secondary sources include historical analyses, law journal articles, book excerpts, and magazine articles. Each book also includes several features to facilitate research, including a bibliography, an annotated table of contents, an annotated list of relevant Supreme Court cases, an introduction, and an index. These elements help to make the Bill of Rights series a fascinating and useful tool for examining the fundamental liberties of American democracy.

In December 1965 in Des Moines, Iowa, John Tinker, then age fifteen, and his sister Mary Beth, thirteen, went to school wearing black armbands as a statement of protest against American military actions in Vietnam. After they refused to remove the bands when asked by school administrators, the students were suspended under a new school policy that banned such armbands. The story might have ended there, but what could have been a minor and forgotten incident instead became a landmark legal case. The Tinker children and their parents challenged the policy in court, and after several years their case was eventually argued before the highest court in the country, the U.S. Supreme Court. The case of *Tinker v. Des Moines* is one small episode in the long history of one of America's basic civil liberties—the right of free speech. Their story features many of the recurring central issues and ideas in the evolution of free speech in America as protected by the First Amendment to the U.S. Constitution.

The heart of the Tinkers' legal challenge to school officials was that their policy violated the free speech clause of the First Amendment, which reads, in part, "Congress shall make no law . . . abridging the freedom of speech." The amendment has roots in English law and history, Enlightenment philosophy, and colonial experience. England's history from the sixteenth through the eighteenth centuries was in part a struggle against despotic kings for individual liberty and democratic government. The ideas on free speech developed during this period by English writers and philosophers such as John Milton and John Locke later influenced James Madison, Thomas Jefferson, and other key founders. Madison championed the power of reason and debate in both governing and the search for truth; he therefore argued that government acts restricting speech and open debate were fundamentally wrong.

Despite the existence of the First Amendment, government officials and other people of authority, such as the school officials in the *Tinker* case, have often acted to control or limit speech. This has been a recurring pattern throughout American history. As early as 1798, seven years after the Bill of Rights was ratified, Congress passed a law that essentially outlawed criticism of the federal government (the law expired in 1801). In the nineteenth century, state and local governments passed numerous laws banning obscenity, blasphemy, and controversial literature, including abolitionist writings. That pattern of repression continued in the twentieth century. Many people, including notable figures such as Margaret Sanger and Emma Goldman, were arrested and jailed for speaking out on controversial topics such as birth control and socialism. Trade union meetings were banned, and people were arrested for membership in groups deemed radical by the government. The actions of school officials in the *Tinker* case, while not as extreme, were consistent with this general pattern.

The Supreme Court's Role

The fact that John and Mary Beth Tinker were able to appeal to judges, up to the Supreme Court, illustrates another important aspect of First Amendment history. Supreme Court involvement in First Amendment cases was not a given in America's first century; the Supreme Court would most likely not have gotten involved in the *Tinker* case if it had happened a century or half century earlier. From 1791 until the early twentieth century, the courts held that the First Amendment's wording ("Congress shall make no law") meant that its free speech protections applied only to actions of the federal government. But beginning in the 1920s, the Supreme Court has ruled that freedom of speech and other First Amendment freedoms of press, religion, and assembly should be recognized as fundamental rights under the Fourteenth Amendment to the Constitution. That amendment, which was ratified in 1868 following the Civil War, states that "Nor shall any State deprive any person of life, liberty, or property, without due process of law." The Supreme Court has interpreted the "due process" clause to expand the First Amendment's protection of free speech against actions by state and local governments—including the school authorities involved in the *Tinker* case. In arguing for the inclusion of free speech as a fundamental right, Benjamin Cardozo, a Supreme Court associate justice from 1932 to 1938, wrote that freedom of speech was "the matrix, the indispensable condition, of nearly every other form of freedom."

Defining Speech

Determining that freedom of speech is a fundamental right that applied to state and local governments was just a first step. In *Tinker v. Des Moines*, the justices of the Supreme Court grappled with several other recurring issues that appear time and again in the history of free speech. One is the question as to what constitutes "speech." Much has changed since the First Amendment was ratified in 1791 in how ideas and feelings are expressed. Speech has grown to consist not only of soapbox lectures and printed handbills, but to also include motion pictures and Internet communications. In addition to coping with changing technologies, the Supreme Court has had to decide whether speech means only words or whether nonverbal expression should also be protected. In the 1931 case of *Stromberg v. California*, the Supreme Court ruled that some actions could be seen as symbolic speech or expressive conduct (that case involved a law prohibiting the displaying of red flags). In the 1968 case of *United States v. O'Brien*, however, the Court held that burning a draft card was not protected speech under the First Amendment. In the *Tinker* case, the court ultimately held that the students were trying to convey a message in wearing the armband and that suspending them did punish them for speech (more recent symbolic speech cases have involved burning the American flag and burning a cross on a person's yard).

Another recurring debate involves what sort of limits should be placed on speech. Even Justice Hugo Black, an associate justice from 1937 to 1971 who was known for his "absolutist" position that "no law meant no law" when it came to interpreting the First Amendment, conceded in his dissenting opinion in *Tinker* that the amendment's clause does not mean that any and all speech could be permitted. "While I have always believed that under the First and Fourteenth Amendments neither the State nor the Federal Government has any authority to regulate or censor the content of speech, I have never believed that any person has a right to give speeches or engage in demonstrations where he pleases and when he pleases." Associate Justice Oliver W. Holmes provided a more famous example in 1919 when he wrote, "The most stringent protection of free speech would not protect a man in falsely shouting fire in a theatre and causing a panic." Over the course of time the Supreme Court has developed various tests and limits that attempt to balance the individual's right of free speech against the government's interest in ensuring a public good. They have justified free speech restrictions against obscenity, defamation, "fighting words" that cause violence, and the advocacy of illegal acts.

A Question of Balance

In the *Tinker* case, lawyers for the school district attempted to justify their armbands policy as a necessary step to prevent disruption in the classroom and distraction from the school's primary purpose of teaching the young. The lawyer for the Tinkers, Dan Johnson, accepted the premise that speech that was truly disruptive was rightfully banned— "marching in the hallway, or standing up in the class and making a speech about the war in Vietnam during mathematics class" is something "the court can prohibit"—but he questioned whether the silent bearing of armbands was disruptive enough. The majority of court justices agreed. Associate Justice Abe Fortas, author of the court opinion, said that student speech that "would materially and substantially disrupt" the classroom was not protected, but that the actions of the Tinkers did not rise to that level. A mere "fear of disturbance," Fortas wrote, "is not enough to overcome the right to freedom of expression."

The students who asserted their right to free expression in the *Tinker v. Des Moines* case are illustrative of another recurring motif in American history—the existence of brave people willing to risk social opprobrium and worse in standing up for what they believe to be their fundamental right of free speech. Recollecting her experiences years later, Mary Beth Tinker talked about receiving threats and having paint thrown at her house. In one case, she remembered:

> I was leaving for school one morning, on my way out the door, and the phone rang and I picked it up. This woman said, "Is this Mary Tinker?" And I said yes. And she said, "I'm going to *kill* you!" At that time, I started a policy I still have today; it's a habit. When anyone calls, I always find out who it is before I talk to them, because of that happening that one morning. It's made me a lot more hardened in certain ways, when you learn in a personal way what the repercussions are for doing unpopular things.

What the Tinkers experienced was far from an isolated incident; many activists asserting their free speech rights throughout American history have been treated worse. However, law professor and First Amendment scholar Rodney Smolla makes the argument that despite the frequent unpopularity of specific cases and free speech plaintiffs, the ideal of free speech itself over the past decades has become a cherished American value:

> While undoubtedly any one decision will often be controversial with the public, which may be deeply divided on topics such as flag-burning or sex on the Internet, on balance what is extraordinary about the evolution of freedom of speech in America over the last 50 years is that it has taken such a strong hold on the American consciousness. . . . This is not to say that in some simplistic sense everybody in America believes in freedom of speech, and certainly it is not to say that everybody in America believes that freedom of speech means the same thing. But it is to say that in a sense both deep and wide, "freedom of speech" is a value that has become powerfully internalized by the American polity. Freedom of speech is a core American belief, almost a kind of secular religious tenet, an article of constitutional faith.

Such "faith" can be read in a 1997 poll by Kenneth Dautrich of the Center for Survey Research and Analysis at the University of Connecticut. The poll found that most Americans still believe, at least in general principle, in the importance of free speech, with 93 percent agreeing with the statement that "it's dangerous to restrict freedom of speech because restricting the freedom of one person could lead to restrictions on everybody."

The Evolution of Free Speech

Tinker v. Des Moines is one of numerous cases that shaped how free speech has evolved in the United States. The selections in this volume examine the circumstances of the creation of the First Amendment and its subsequent legal history. The writings include rulings by Supreme Court justices, analyses by legal historians, and accounts of how the First Amendment has affected people's lives. The selections demonstrate both the attraction many Americans have toward the free speech ideal and the controversies of its application. Perhaps an appropriate final word comes from Justice Fortas's *Tinker v. Des Moines* decision: "Any word spoken, in class, in the lunchroom, or on the campus, that deviates from the views of another person may start an argument or cause a disturbance," he wrote. "But our Constitution says we must take this risk . . . and our history says that it is this sort of hazardous freedom—this kind of openness—that is the basis of our national strength and of the independence and vigor of Americans who grow up and live in this relatively permissive, often disputatious, society."

CHAPTER ONE

Free Speech in Early American History

The Bill of Rights

The Origins and Early Development of Free Speech in the United States

Michael Kahn

Michael Kahn is an attorney in Melbourne, Florida, and is vice chair of the First Amendment Law Committee of the Public Interest Law Section of the Florida Bar. He is also an adjunct professor at Rollins College in Winter Park, Florida. In the following selection he provides a brief overview of the early history of the First Amendment's clause protecting free speech. The people who wrote the Constitution and the Bill of Rights were influenced by English law and history as well as the "natural rights" philosophy being developed in Europe in the seventeenth and eighteenth centuries. But the passage of the First Amendment did not prevent the new national government from passing laws punishing people for seditious libel (speech construed as fomenting rebellion against the government) in 1798. The First Amendment's freedom of speech provisions had little impact on the first hundred years of U.S. legal history, Kahn concludes.

The First Amendment guaranty of freedom of speech is one of the most revered cornerstones of American society. The full text of the amendment reads: "Congress shall make no law respecting an establishment of religion or prohibiting the free exercise thereof, or abridging the freedom of speech or of the press or of the right of the people peaceably to assemble and to petition the government for a redress of grievances." . . .

Most scholars agree that the American political concept of free speech as embodied in the First Amendment originated

Michael Kahn, "The Origination and Early Development of Free Speech in the United States: A Brief Overview," *Florida Bar Journal*, vol. 76, October 2002, p. 71. Copyright © 2002 by The Florida Bar. Reproduced by permission.

with the British. However, in the 17th and 18th centuries the intellectual heritage of free speech was diverse. The 17th century Dutch philosopher Benedict de Spinoza (1632–1677), whose philosophy was well known in the colonies, believed that liberty of speech was based upon an "indefeasible natural right" of individuals. Spinoza qualified his support of liberty of speech with the caveat that in some instances government could punish speech if a man spoke opinions "which by their very nature nullify the [social] compact." The French philosopher Montesquieu (1689–1755) believed in the distinction between speech and overt action. In his monumental work, *The Spirit of the Laws*, he wrote: "The laws do not take upon them to punish any other than overt acts. . . . Words do not constitute an overt act; they remain only an idea."

Thomas Jefferson drew from the precepts of the British philosopher John Locke when he penned the Declaration of Independence. Locke eloquently spoke of man's inalienable rights to life, liberty, and pursuit of property. He was an adherent of the Social Compact theory of government by which a free and independent man gave up unfettered freedom (and anarchy) for the order and security of civilized government. Thus, in advocating the Social Contract theory, Locke at once established the concept of certain unalienable rights inherent to man as well as a theory of government other than divine right. Further, Locke advocated the right of revolution if the government, established by the consent of the governed, should tyrannize its citizens, thus breaking the contract.

Certainly the understanding of free speech that the framers of the Constitution and the Bill of Rights had was taken largely from the scholarship of Sir William Blackstone. He was one of the most ardent early advocates of free speech and, perhaps, its foremost spokesperson in 18th century England. An oft-quoted passage from Blackstone's *Commentaries on the Law of England* is thought to have formed the basis of the inchoate American colonial concept of free speech. Blackstone observed that

the liberty of the press is indeed essential to the nature of a free state; but this consists in laying no previous restraints upon publication and not in freedom from censure for criminal matter when published. Every free man has an undoubted right to lay what sentiments he pleases before the public; to forbid this is to destroy the freedom of the press; but if he publishes what is improper, mischievous or illegal he must take the consequences of his own temerity.

It is significant to note that Blackstone excepted certain categories of utterances as not being included in protected speech, including speech that was "blasphemous, immoral, treasonable, schismatical, seditious, or scandalous libels." This led to the early distinction which became rooted in American law between prior restraint and subsequent punishment, the definition and elucidation of which distinction an entire series of lectures could easily be composed.

Free Speech in England

Let us not mistake our English forefathers, however; their feet certainly were made of clay. The earliest English history and jurisprudence reveal a deep-seated fear by the church and crown of free speech, which was exacerbated when in 1476 William Caxton set up the first printing press at Westminster and published the first book in England. Authorities of the church and crown worried, probably correctly in retrospect, that the twin "evils" of heresy and insurrection would be furthered by widespread publications and corresponding dissemination of information. Generally speaking, the British crown used three methods to suppress free speech: licensing, constructive treason, and seditious libel. Licensing was the original system of "prior restraint." Soon after the first book was printed in England, the crown empowered the Stationer's Company, whose approval was necessary for publication. An appointed licensor of the Stationer's Company could censor the work and could in his sole discretion deny or approve the license necessary for publication. This system of licensing remained until spring 1695 when the legislation expired not because of any enlightenment with regard to free speech, but because of its impracticality. In 1710, the Statute of Anne first gave to individual authors limited rights to their publications for a period of time.

The legal theories of constructive treason and seditious libel were also utilized to curtail free speech. The law of constructive treason derived from the Statute of 25 Edward III (1352). Constructive treason consisted of either imagining the king's death, levying war against the king, or adhering to his enemies. This law was extended to printed works, with one of the most egregious prosecutions occurring in the case of John Twyn. In a book that he was preparing for publication, Twyn had the temerity to suggest that the king was accountable to the people who were entitled to self government. For this radical notion, he was convicted of constructive treason, hanged, drawn, and quartered.

The seeds of seditious libel originated in a collection of laws known as Scandalum Magnatum, which was passed in 1275 and outlawed any speech that contributed to discord between the king and his people. Sir Edward Coke, as attorney general, reported to the infamous Star Chamber in a case in 1606 that libel of a government official is a greater offense than a private libel and even a true libel may be punished. Coke was another jurisprudential icon of his day, whose work was required reading for 18th century American lawyers, including Thomas Jefferson. The theory behind seditious libel was set forth by Chief Justice Holt in 1704 when he said that "if people should not be called to account for possessing the people with an ill opinion of the government, no government can subsist. For it is very necessary for all governments, that the people should have a good opinion of it." The jury's role in trials for seditious libel was restricted to ascertaining whether the speech was published; judges ruled whether the speech was libelous.

The British colonists who settled America desired to enlarge the right of free speech. The celebrated case of John Peter Zenger in 1735 is representative. He was the publisher of the *New York Weekly Journal* and was charged with seditious libel by the governor of New York. His lawyers, Andrew Hamilton and James Alexander, argued that the truth of his critical statements against the governor general should be a defense and that the jury and not the judge should adjudicate criminal intent. Although these novel (to the British) tenets were rejected by the trial judge, the jury set Zenger free.

In literal and figurative revolt from the oppressive tactics of the British after the Revolution, the young nation expanded the notion of free speech but at the same time the vestiges of English suppression remained. James Madison boldly introduced his original version of the First Amendment in the Bill of Rights in 1789 by stating: "The people shall not be deprived or abridged of their right to speak, to write, or to publish their sentiments; and the freedom of the press, as one of the great bulwarks of liberty, shall be inviolable."

However, some scholars have interpreted early American jurisprudence regarding freedom of speech as nothing more than a reiteration of the Blackstonian concept which embraced the pernicious laws concerning seditious libel. As libertarian and historian Leonard Levy concluded when commenting upon the subject,

> Freedom of speech and press, as all the scattered evidence suggests, was not understood to include a right to broadcast sedition by words. The security of the state against libelous advocacy or attack was always regarded as outweighing any social interest in open expression. . . .

He reluctantly concluded that the First Amendment did not repudiate Blackstone but left the law of seditious libel in force.

The Role of the Founding Fathers

Since we, like all cultures, have idealized our founding forefathers, it may dismay some to realize that the record of the framers of our Constitution is not unblemished with regard to freedom of speech, especially during and immediately after the Revolutionary War. For example, the acknowledged author of the First Amendment, James Madison, did not support a Bill of Rights either when he endeavored to become one of Virginia's first two U.S. senators or when he ran for the House of Representatives. Only after he lost these two elections did a then philosophically enlightened Madison become a staunch supporter of the Bill of Rights. Thomas Jefferson urged state courts to use state sedition laws against his political opponents. With Jefferson's support, the Virginia legislature in

1777 passed a bill requiring "loyalty oaths," the purpose of which was to punish a person who was "a traitor in thought, but not in deed" according to Jefferson. In this endeavor he also had the support of George Washington.

In 1798, the Federalist government of the United States of America passed four related pieces of legislation known as the Alien and Sedition acts, which were reminiscent of British laws proscribing seditious libel. Ostensibly, the legislation was caused by rising tensions with France which many thought foreshadowed war. However, the Federalists also did not care for the level of insult hurled at President Adams and even at the venerable George Washington by the press. The fourth section of the legislation was the infamous Sedition Act, which prohibited the publication of

> false, scandalous, and malicious writing or writings against the government of the United States, or either house of the Congress of the United States, or the president of the United States, with the intent to defame [them]; or to bring them [into] contempt or disrepute.

The act provided that truth would be a defense and that the accused would have the right of a jury trial.

Jefferson, apparently having a change of heart on the subject, and James Madison helped to pass the Virginia and Kentucky resolutions in fierce opposition to the Alien and Sedition acts. In large part his vigorous opposition to the alien and sedition acts led to Jefferson's electoral victory in the hotly contested presidential election of 1800. In his 1801 inaugural address, Jefferson defended the freedom of the press and stressed the necessity of preserving the liberties of thought and speech for all citizens.

After these tumultuous early years in our nation's history, the status of freedom of speech remained fairly quiescent in American jurisprudence for over 100 years.

Free Speech Is the Great Bulwark of Liberty

Cato

John Trenchard and Thomas Gordon were two British lawyers and journalists. From 1720 to 1723, the *London Journal* published a series of their letters under the pen name "Cato"— the name of a statesman of ancient Rome. These articles were later published in book form. While Trenchard and Gordon were minor figures in British politics, their influence was considerable in the American colonies as their letters were widely and repeatedly reprinted in colonial publications. A very young Benjamin Franklin published them in 1722 when his brother was imprisoned by the Massachusetts legislature for criticizing the government.

The fifteenth of these letters, titled "Of Freedom of Speech: That the Same Is Inseparable from Publick Liberty," is excerpted here. Trenchard and Gordon argue that freedom of speech is essential for holding government accountable to the people by permitting honest and accurate criticism of those in authority. Citing historical examples from Roman and English history, they conclude that "freedom of speech is the great Bulwark of liberty"—a phrase later found in the 1776 Virginia Declaration of Rights, which was one of the inspirations of the U.S. Bill of Rights.

Sir,
Without Freedom of Thought, there can be no such Thing as Wisdom; and no such Thing as publick Liberty, without Freedom of Speech: Which is the Right of every Man, as far as by it he does not hurt and control the Right of another,

Cato, "Of Freedom of Speech: That the Same Is Inseparable from Publick Liberty," *London Journal*, February 4, 1720.

and this is the only Check which it ought to suffer, the only Bounds which it ought to know.

This sacred Privilege is so essential to free Government, that the Security of Property, and the Freedom of Speech, always go together; and in those wretched Countries where a Man cannot call his Tongue his own, he can scarce call any Thing else his own. Whoever would overthrow the Liberty of the Nation, must begin by subduing the Freedom of Speech; a Thing terrible to publick Traytors.

This Secret was so well known to the Court of King Charles I, that his wicked Ministry procured a Proclamation to forbid the People to talk of Parliaments, which those Traytors had laid aside. To assert the undoubted Right of the Subject, and defend his Majesty's Legal Prerogative, was called disaffection, and punished as Sedition. . . .

That Men ought to speak well of their Governors, is true, while their Governors deserve to be well spoken of; but to do publick Mischief, without hearing of it, is only the Prerogative and Felicity of Tyranny: A free People will be shewing that they are so, by their Freedom of Speech.

The Administration of Government is nothing else, but the Attendance of the Trustees of the People upon the Interest and Affairs of the People. And as it is the Part and Business of the People, for whose Sake alone all publick Matters are, or ought to be, transacted, to see whether they be will or ill transacted; so it is the Interest, and ought to be the Ambition, of all honest Magistrates, to have their Deeds openly examined, and publickly scanned: Only the wicked Governors of Men dread what is said of them. . . .

A Symptom of Good Government

Freedom of Speech is ever the Symptom, as well as the Effect, of good Government. In old Rome, all was left to the Judgement and Pleasure of the People; who examined the publick Proceedings with such Discretion, and censured those who administered them with such Equity and Mildness, that in the Space of Three Hundred Years, not Five publick Ministers suffered unjustly. Indeed, whenever the Commons proceeded to Violence, the Great Ones had been the Aggressors.

Guilt only dreads Liberty of Speech, which drags it out of its lurking Holes, and exposes its Deformity and Horror to Day-light. *Horatius, Valerius, Cincinnatus*, and other virtuous and undesigning Magistrates of the *Roman* Commonwealth, had nothing to fear from Liberty of Speech. Their virtuous Administration, the more it was examined, the more it brightened and gained by Enquiry. When *Valerius*, in particular, was accused, upon some slight Grounds, of affecting the Diadem; he, who was the first Minister of Rome, did not accuse the People for examining his Conduct, but approved his Innocence in a Speech to them; he gave such Satisfaction to them, and gained such Popularity to himself, that they gave him a new Name; *inde cognomen factum Publicolae est*; to denote that he was their Favourite and their Friend. . . .

But Things afterward took another Turn: Rome, with the Loss of its Liberty, lost also the Freedom of its Speech; then Mens Words began to be feared and watched; then first began the poisonous Race of Informers, banished indeed under the righteous Administration of *Titus, Nerva, Trajan, Aurelius* &c. but encouraged and enriched by the vile Ministry of *Sejanus, Tigellinus, Pallas*, and *Cleander*. . . .

The best Princes have ever encouraged and promoted Freedom of Speech; they knew that upright Measures would defend themselves, and that all upright Men would defend them. Tacitus, speaking of the Reigns of some of the Princes above-mention'd, says with Extasy, *Rara temporum felicitate, ubi sentire quae velis & quae sentias dicere liceat*: A blessed Time, when you might think what you would, and speak what you thought! . . .

A Bulwark of Liberty

Freedom of Speech is the great Bulwark of Liberty; they prosper and die together: And it is the Terror of Traytors and Oppressors, and a Barrier against them. It produces excellent Writers, and encourages Men of fine Genius. *Tacitus* tells us, that the *Roman* Commonwealth bred great and numerous Authors, who writ with equal Boldness and Elloquence: But when it was enslaved, those great Wits were no more. . . . Tyranny had usurped the Place of Equality, which is the Soul of Liberty, and destroyed publick Courage. The Minds of Men, terrified by unjust Power, degenerated into all the Vileness and Methods of Servitude: Abject Sycophancy and blind Submission grew the only means of Preferment, and indeed of Safety; Men durst not open their Mouths, but to flatter. . . .

All Ministers, therefore, who were Oppressors, or intended to be Oppressors, have been loud in their Complaints against Freedom of Speech, and the Licence of the Press, and always restrained, or endeavoured to restrain, both. In consequence of this, they have brow-beaten Writers, punished them violently, and against Law, and burnt their Works. By all which they shewed how much Truth alarmed them, and how much they were at Enmity with Truth. . . .

Freedom of Speech, therefore, being of such infinite Importance to the Preservation of Liberty, everyone who loves Liberty ought to encourage Freedom of Speech. . . .

God be thanked, we Englishmen have neither lost our Liberties, nor are in Danger of losing them. Let us always cherish this matchless Blessing, almost peculiar to ourselves; that our Posterity may, many Ages hence, ascribe their Freedom to our Zeal. The Defence of Liberty is a noble, a heavenly Office; which can only be performed where Liberty is.

Myths About America's Founders and Free Speech

Eugene Volokh

Some libertarians and conservatives have criticized modern judges for applying their own values in interpreting the First Amendment in ways that restrict freedom of speech contrary to what America's founders intended. In this selection, law professor Eugene Volokh argues that such views are based on historical myths rather than historical fact. The people who wrote the First Amendment had a much narrower conception of free speech than is accepted today, he contends. For much of American history, he argues, the First Amendment did not prevent laws providing criminal punishment against people who engaged in antigovernment or obscene speech. Volokh teaches First Amendment law at the law school of the University of California, Los Angeles. His writings include the book *The First Amendment: Law, Cases, Problems, and Policy Arguments.*

The liberals on the Supreme Court, and in universities, have been undermining the Framers' First Amendment handiwork. . . . And this loss of liberty stems from liberals' disdain for the text of the Constitution, and liberal judges' willingness to make law, instead of simply applying it. Soon we will lose the freedom of speech that Americans have long taken for granted.

That's the story I've been hearing from many of my conservative and libertarian correspondents. And it's just plain false.

History of the First Amendment

1. *First Amendment history*. To begin with, it's false because it rests on myths about the past. For most of American history, speech was less constitutionally protected than it is today. There was never a time when "no law" meant "no law" and all speech was protected.

In the late 1700s, it wasn't even clear whether the First Amendment covered criminal punishment for politically incorrect speech. Many people argued that it applied only to "prior restraints," such as injunctions or prepublication censorship rule. Laws criminalizing speech after it's published, the argument went, were perfectly constitutional—even if, for instance, the laws banned criticism of the government. Only in the 1930s was it firmly settled that the First Amendment protects speech against criminal punishment.

In the late 1700s and early 1800s, courts routinely held that some antigovernment speech—even speech that wasn't directly inciting crime—was constitutionally unprotected. In many states, until the 1810s and 1820s truth wasn't a defense to criminal libel prosecutions. Even when it became a defense, it generally applied only when the statement was made with "good motives" and for "justifiable ends," however a judge or jury chose to interpret these vague phrases. Those limitations weren't eliminated until the 1960s.

In the first half of the 1800s, courts held that blasphemy could be outlawed, and blasphemy covered not just swearing but the offensive public denial of the truth of Christianity. Until the mid-1900s, judges routinely sent people to jail for publishing newspaper articles that criticized the judges' decisions. Until the mid-1900s, obscenity laws punished not just hard-core pornography, but serious literature as well as discussion of contraceptives. . . .

Modern free-speech protections were largely the work of Justices Oliver Wendell Holmes and Louis D. Brandeis, who were generally associated with the liberal wing of the Court on most issues; of FDR's [President Franklin D. Roosevelt] liberal appointees to the Court; and of the notoriously liberal Warren Court. On today's [2004] Supreme Court, conservative Justices Anthony Kennedy and Clarence Thomas take a broad view of free speech, often broader than many of their liberal colleagues. But until the late 1980s, conservatives generally took the narrower view, not just on matters such as sex and flag desecration, but even on political and social advocacy.

Interpreting the Text

2. *First Amendment text.* Nor are conservatives somehow inherently more pro-free-speech because of their respect for constitutional text. The text of the First Amendment sounds categorical—"Congress shall make no law . . . abridging the freedom of speech, or of the press"—but it can't be taken as a literal protection of all speech, all the time. Is Congress forbidden from restricting the use of loudspeakers in residential D.C. neighborhoods? Do people have a constitutional right to send death threats to the president, or publicly threaten other forms of terrorism? Would it be unconstitutional for Congress to provide that federal employees can lose their statutory civil-service protection for hurling insults at each other, or at patrons?

What about copyright laws, which restrict the right of the press to publish the words that it wants to publish? The First Amendment has been applied to the states, via the Fourteenth Amendment. Are states barred from enacting laws punishing libel, or false advertising?

Now there are ways to explain why these restrictions are constitutional. For instance, restricting the use of loudspeakers regulates the noise that speech causes, and not its content. Death threats, even if they aren't accompanied by any actual violence, aren't a valuable contribution to public debate, and are potentially very harmful. But while these are sensible distinctions, it's hardly mandated by the text. We can't just say "no law means no law" and resolve the problems that way. . . .

What Judges Do

3. *Making up the law.* This also shows the error of faulting liberal judges for "making up the law" in this area. Unfortunately, the First Amendment is so general that judges have to

create legal rules that turn the broad words into concretely applicable law. Judges can't just rely on the text. They can't just rely on the original meaning, which is highly ambiguous. (As I mentioned, the Framers didn't even agree whether the First Amendment applied to subsequent punishments, or only to prior restraints.)

One can criticize judges for just making up constitutional guarantees that aren't mentioned in the Constitution at all. But here the Constitution does say something—but something very general. If it's to be enforced at all, judges have to give it specific meaning. And that's been part of our constitutional tradition since shortly after the Framing. Conservative and liberal judges alike have done this, as to various constitutional provisions, because they have to do it.

I'm delighted that many modern conservatives take a broad view of the First Amendment. But such a view shouldn't rest on myths about American history, about the supposed clarity of the constitutional text, or about the possibility of judges simply following the law, without making law in the process.

Free Speech in the Nineteenth Century

Thomas L. Tedford

Thomas L. Tedford is professor emeritus of communication at the University of North Carolina at Greensboro. He is the author of the book *Freedom of Speech in the United States*, excerpted here. Tedford provides a broad overview of freedom of speech in the United States in the years between 1798 and 1917. He argues that during this time Americans often found their freedom of speech restricted by the government at the national, state, and local levels. The Alien and Sedition Acts of 1798 punished "writing, printing, uttering or publishing any false, scandalous, and malicious writing . . . against the government of the United States." Although the acts expired in 1800, state and local laws against "sedition" were directed against abolitionists, union organizers, and other people deemed threatening to the social order. In addition, state and federal laws criminalized speech deemed as either blasphemy or obscenity. The Supreme Court did little to enforce the First Amendment's guarantees of free speech during this time, Tedford concludes, arguing that it treated the First Amendment with "benign neglect."

The First Amendment's command that "Congress shall make no law . . . abridging the freedom of speech" seems clear; unfortunately it is not, as witnessed by the hundreds of essays, books, editorials, debates, and legal opinions on the subject. Furthermore, numerous laws have been passed at both the state and federal levels to proscribe the communication freedoms of American citizens. The disparity between

Thomas L. Tedford, *Freedom of Speech in the United States*. Carbondale: Southern Illinois University Press, 1985. Copyright © 1985 by Random House, Inc. Reproduced by permission.

principle and practice is grounded in history, for even the Founding Fathers were in disagreement about how to interpret the specifics of the Bill of Rights—the First Amendment in particular. Near the conclusion of his carefully documented study in *Freedom of Speech and Press in Early American History*, Leonard Levy remarks that the nation's founders were "sharply divided and possessed no clear understanding" of what they meant by freedom of speech. Levy's finding is confirmed when both common law and statutory constraints upon content are examined for the period of 1791 to the Espionage Acts of World War I. As if to show complete agreement with the English view that freedom of speech existed when there was an absence of prior restraint (but that punishment could be inflicted *after* publication), Americans celebrated their newfound liberty by proceeding to prosecute at common law, or by newly passed statute law, speech thought to be seditious, defamatory, or blasphermous.

Seditious Libel

In the summer of 1789, just a few days before the Congress passed the first of the alien and sedition bills, Thomas Jefferson described the increasing efforts of the Federalists[1] to punish their political opponents as a "reign of witches." . . .

Although the Alien Acts were not vigorously enforced, the opposite was true of the Sedition Act of 1798. This law, which provided penalties for "writing, printing, uttering or publishing any false, scandalous and malicious writing . . . against the government of the United States," was enthusiastically prosecuted, particularly in the New England and mid-Atlantic states, where Federalists were in control. At least twenty-four Republican editors, one congressman, and a number of private citizens were prosecuted under the Sedition Act, including Benjamin Bache, grandson of Benjamin Franklin and editor of the leading Republican paper, the Philadelphia *Aurora*; editors of the Boston *Independent Chronicle*, the New York *Argus*, the Richmond *Examiner*,

1. The Federalist Party and Thomas Jefferson's Democrat-Republican Party were the first two organized political parties in the United States.

and the Baltimore *American*; and Republican Congressman Matthew Lyon, who had publicly criticized President Adams. In addition, the *Time Piece* and the *Mount Pleasant Register*, both anti-Federalist newspapers in New York, ceased publication as a result of the prosecutions, while in New London, Connecticut, the *Bee* suspended publication for five months in 1800 while its editor served time in prison for sedition.

In a comic episode that was counterproductive to the Federalist cause, an intoxicated Luther Baldwin of Newark, New Jersey, articulated his opinion of the controversy—within hearing distance of Federalist sympathizers—by saying that he didn't care if someone fired a cannon through President Adams' ass! For this remark Baldwin was arrested, tried, and convicted for speaking seditious words "tending to defame the President and Government of the United States." Upon conviction he was fined, assessed court costs, and placed in a federal jail until the fine and court fees were paid. With wicked glee the Republican press told the nation of the conviction of this "dangerous" drunkard, and within days the now sober fellow became a hero to the Jeffersonians. Continuing the attack, the New York *Argus* dryly assured its readers that Baldwin was no real danger to the president, for no person would think of "firing at such a disgusting a target" as the ass of John Adams.

The constitutional issues inherent in the Alien and Sedition Acts never reached the Supreme Court during the years the laws were in force, although a number of Federalist judges in lower courts (including three Supreme Court justices who were hearing cases in circuit courts) did rule that the acts did not violate the Constitution. Popular opposition to the legislation was a factor in the defeat of the Federalists in the election of 1800. The newly elected President Jefferson soon pardoned all those convicted under the Alien and Sedition Acts. However, this first free-speech crisis in the new republic clearly demonstrates the tenuous health of the First Amendment at the beginning of the nineteenth century, soon reconfirmed by events that led to the war between the states.

Freedom of Speech and the Slavery Question

The suppression of "sedition" before, during, and after the Civil War focused upon two types of messages: those that urged freedom and justice for blacks and those wartime messages that were critical of the government, whether of the Union or of the Confederacy. During the 1820s, debates over slavery became more and more heated; by the early 1830s, abolitionists began to organize societies so that they could speak effectively against the evils of involuntary servitude. Predictably, the legislatures of the southern states responded with laws designed to punish the communication of abolitionist arguments.

The Virginia Act of 1836 is typical of the restraints placed upon freedom of speech by the southern states. The statute begins by acknowledging the source of the subversive opinion as "certain abolition and anti-slavery societies and evil disposed persons, being and residing in some of the non-slaveholding states." Article 1 then provides that any member or agent of an abolitionist society who comes to Virginia to advocate "by speaking or writing, that the owners of slaves have no property in the same," or to "advise the abolition of slavery," is guilty of a high misdemeanor. Such persons, upon conviction, could be punished by a fine of $200 and imprisoned for up to three years.

Meanwhile, many conservatives in the North, partly from prejudice and partly from a belief that northerners should "mind their own business," did what they could to discourage the work of the antislavery organizations. This attitude was reversed to a great degree during the late 1830s and early 1840s in response to harsh antiabolitionist legislation in the South and mob violence against opponents of slavery in both. North and South. . . .

After the Civil War began, officials in both the Union and the Confederacy permitted a surprising degree of freedom of expression, although there were notable exceptions in both camps. . . .

The Constitution of the Confederate States of America, ratified on March 29, 1861, included a freedom-of-speech clause identical in language to that of the First Amendment to the U.S. Constitution. However, this did not prohibit the government, the military, and some private citizens exercising extralegal constraints from attempting to control seditious speech during the war. . . .

Freedom of Speech After the Civil War

During the years between the conclusion of the Civil War and the turn of the century, the most sustained restraint upon sedition occurred in the South, where a combination of economic pressure and organized terror effectively eliminated almost all civil rights advocacy on behalf of blacks. . . .

Meanwhile, the growth of the labor movement and the attraction which that phenomenon had for a variety of radical anarchists, socialists, and other antiestablishment groups resulted in the passage of laws similar to those enacted during the sedition controversy of one hundred years earlier. This time, however, the repressive legislation was approved, not by the United States Congress but by the legislatures of a number of *states*. Starting with the strike against the McCormick Harvester Company in 1886 and the bomb explosion and riot in Chicago's Haymarket Square during a rally in support of that strike, many state officials expressed alarm at the "seditious activities" of union organizers and their radical supporters. The issue became one of national concern when President William McKinley was assassinated by anarchist Leon Czolgosz in September of 1901.

In 1905 the Industrial Workers of the World (or IWW; nicknamed the "Wobblies") organized for the express purpose of abolishing capitalism and forming the working people of America into a Marxist-type industrial society. To get their message to the workers, the Wobblies spoke in the streets and in other open places where groups of lumbermen, migrant workers, or factory employees could be found. Attempts by employers and local police to censor the Wobblies caused numerous free-speech confrontations in communities from coast to coast. Consequently, the IWW was driven to make the First Amendment a key issue in its organizational campaigns. Local officials all too often ignored their oath to uphold the Constitution of the United States and assaulted, imprisoned, starved, and even tortured advocates of the Wobbly philosophy. Finally, the IWW movement was destroyed by a series of raids conducted by the federal government soon after America entered World War I.

Because of labor and social unrest in some parts of the country during the four decades preceding World War I, a number of states including New York. New Jersey, Wisconsin, and California passed antisedition statutes of their own. These state sedition acts are called *criminal anarchy* or *criminal syndicalism* laws. In general, their purpose is to punish at the state level what the Alien and Sedition Acts of 1798, and, later, the federal Espionage Acts of 1917 and 1918 sought to punish at the national level. . . .

Free Speech and Blasphemy

In an English blasphemy case of 1676, presiding judge Lord Hale announced that "Christianity being parcel of the laws of England, therefore to reproach the Christian religion is to speak in subversion of the law." This view, widely accepted by English and American colonial judges, was confirmed by Lord Mansfield in a 1767 decision in which he wrote: "The eternal principles of natural religion are part of the common law; the essential principles of revealed religion are part of the common law; so that any person reviling, subverting, or ridiculing them may be prosecuted at common law." Following the American Revolution, this tradition concerning blasphemy was accepted in many state courts, as were the common-law traditions governing seditious libel and private libel. Although a number of states did codify antiblasphemy laws, others simply used the common law to punish those whose speech "maliciously reviled God or religion." For years, the First Amendment's assurances of freedom of speech, and of the separation of church and state, had little deterrent effect upon pious prosecutors, judges, and jurors. . . .

Harold Nelson states in his introduction to *Freedom of the Press from Hamilton to the Warren Court* that about two dozen blasphemy cases are reported for the nineteenth century. . . .

Although this was by no means a "reign of terror" against religious dissent, the trial records do serve as a reminder of how the First Amendment was ignored by many government officials. In contemporary times the religio-moral offense of blasphemy is rarely prosecuted. . . .

Obscenity

While attempts to suppress blasphemy remained few in number and in the twentieth century have all but ceased, the opposite is true for speech thought to be sexually immoral or "impure"—expression labeled under the common law as "obscene." In the years before the Civil War, as happened during the colonial period, there were few arrests for "obscenity"; those which did occur were at the state level. The first trial resulting from such an arrest took place in 1815 in Philadelphia, Pennsylvania, when Jesse Sharpless was charged and convicted under the common law (there were as yet no state or federal obscenity statutes) for exhibiting "for money, to persons . . . a certain lewd, wicked, scandalous, infamous, and obscene painting, representing a man in an obscene, impudent, and indecent posture with a woman." Six years later the Supreme Court of Massachusetts upheld the common-law conviction of Peter Holmes for publishing John Cleland's *Memoirs of a Woman of Pleasure* (also known as *Fanny Hill*) because the book was "lewd, wicked, scandalous, infamous and obscene." At about this time, the states began to write the common law of obscene libel into the statute books. Franklyn S. Haiman notes in *Freedom of Speech* that Vermont was the first state to codify the law of obscenity, doing so in 1821. Connecticut adopted an antiobscenity statute in 1834, and Massachusetts followed with a similar act in 1835. Eventually, all of the states approved laws against obscenity, although definitions and details varied from state to state. However, unlike what happened with private libel and the religio-moral offense of blasphemy—both of which were omitted from the federal criminal code—the United States government soon entered the arena of sexual censorship.

In 1842 Congress passed the first federal obscenity statute in the form of Section 28 of the Tariff Act. This section barred the "importation of all indecent and obscene prints, paintings, lithographs, engravings and transparencies" into the United States. It has been amended several times to add items such as photographs, films, and phonograph records to the list. . . . The second federal censorship law was the Postal Act of March 3, 1865, Section 16 of which declares that "no obscene book, pamphlet, picture, print, or other publication of a vulgar and indecent character, shall be admitted into the mails of the United States." . . . Neither of these early laws defined "obscenity," nor did they provide enforcement machinery. Consequently, there was for a time little organized federal censorship, a fact which in the early 1870s became an obsessive concern of a young, puritanical retail clerk in New York City—Anthony Comstock.

A veteran of the Civil War and in his early twenties, Anthony Comstock arrived in New York City in 1867. There, he secured a job as a clerk in a dry-goods store. So disturbed was Comstock by the reading materials passed around by his fellow employees that he tracked down one supplier of "indecent literature" and had him arrested. Encouraged by this success, he determined to rid the city of all such "filth," and with a zeal unequaled in American history became the nation's premier crusader against "vice." In 1873, at the age of twenty-eight, he successfully enlisted the support of several prominent New Yorkers, including financier J.P. Morgan and soap magnate Samuel Colgate, in founding the New York YMCA's Committee for the Suppression of Vice (later to be renamed the New York Society for the Suppression of Vice). As news of this development spread, procensorship Watch and Ward Societies were formed in numerous communities throughout the United States.

Also in 1873, Comstock almost singlehandedly lobbied through Congress a detailed statute to prohibit the mailing of "obscene" communications or any materials concerning birth control or abortion. Later, as an unpaid postal inspector, he worked evangelistically to help enforce the new law. . . .

Two cases decided by the U.S. Supreme Court in 1896 complete the system of restraint placed upon sexual expression prior to World War I. In the first case, the conviction of New York publisher Lew Rosen for mailing "indecent" pictures of females in violation of the Comstock Act was upheld by the Supreme Court. In its decision, the Supreme Court accepted the trial judge's use of Lord Cockburn's ruling in the 1868 English case of *Regina v. Hicklin*, which defines "obscenity" as that which has a tendency "to deprave and corrupt those whose minds are open to such immoral influences, and into whose hands a publication of this sort may fall." Consequently, this "most susceptible person" standard became the accepted one in both federal and state courts throughout the nation during the first thirty years of the twentieth century.

In the second case, the Supreme Court overturned the conviction of Dan K. Swearingen, who had been found guilty in a federal district court of Kansas of mailing a newspaper that contained an "obscene, lewd, and lascivious" article. The offending piece charged an unnamed—but, evidently, a readily identifiable—person with being a "red headed mental and physical bastard," and a "black hearted coward" who would "sell a mother's honor with less hesitancy and for much less silver than Judas betrayed the Saviour, and who would pimp and fatten on a sister's shame with as much unction as a buzzard gluts in carrion." While agreeing that the language was extreme, the Supreme Court ruled that no obscenity was involved. "Obscenity," said the Court, does not apply to words that are simply "coarse and vulgar," but it does concern language addressing "that form of immorality which has relation to sexual impurity."

Although the Supreme Court's *Rosen* and *Swearingen* decisions are not "landmark cases" in the legal sense, they are milestones in the evolutionary development of controls upon sexual speech. In *Rosen*, the Court interpreted the Comstock Act so as to make it illegal in the United States to mail anything that a jury might find sexually provocative to a child. And in Swearingen, the Court—without realizing it—climaxed three centuries of evolution of the Anglo-American concept of the "obscene." That which began as a seventeenth-century church punishment for the sin of communicating an immoral or blasphemous thought had now become the state crime of communicating an erotic one. . . .

Constraints of Time, Place, and Manner

In 1897 the U.S. Supreme Court decided a case of time, place, and manner which served as legal precedent on the use of public places for speechmaking until it was overruled by a more liberal Court in 1939. The case was *Davis v. Massachusetts*—often called the Boston Common case—that began when minister William F. Davis preached a sermon on the Common of the City of Boston without a permit as was required by law. For this, Davis was fined and required to pay court costs. The Massachusetts Supreme Court upheld the conviction.

Upon appeal to the U.S. Supreme Court, Davis argued that his First Amendment rights had been violated and that the law under which he had been convicted was unconstitutional. The Supreme Court rejected the minister's claim and upheld the constitutionality of the Boston ordinance. In so ruling, the Court said that government was entrusted with the supervision of public places and had complete control over their use, including their use for speechmaking. "For the legislature absolutely or conditionally to forbid public speaking in a highway or public park," said the Court, "is no more an infringement of the rights of a member of the public than for the owner of a private house to forbid it in his house." Forty-two years would pass before the High Court would liberalize this restrictive decision.

Benign Neglect of the First Amendment

In summary, despite the ratification of the First Amendment, government at either the national or state level attempted to control the public communication of aliens, women, and blacks during the first 130 years of the republic. The English common law concerning forbidden expression was accepted to a large degree in the United States, so that in one form or another laws were enforced to punish sedition, defamation, and the religio-moral "crimes" of blasphemy and obscenity. Although licensing of the press was a dead issue, other forms of media and channel constraints were practiced, including copyright, import and mail restrictions, and the licensing of radio transmitters, beginning with the Radio Act of 1912.

Governmental units were given support in the control of speechmaking in public places by the Supreme Court's decision of 1897 upholding a Boston ordinance requiring that a permit be secured before a public place was used for speaking. Throughout this time of national ferment, which included the Civil War, the U.S. Supreme Court treated the First Amendment with benign neglect, announcing no "ringing defenses" of the revolutionary command which initiates the nation's Bill of Rights: "Congress shall make no law . . . abridging freedom of speech, or of the press."

CHAPTER TWO

Balancing Free Speech, Community Order, and National Security

The Bill of Rights

The Supreme Court Grapples with Free Speech and Sedition

Robert S. Peck

Robert S. Peck is the president of the Center for Constitutional Litigation, a Washington, D.C., law firm. He is also an adjunct professor of law at American University and George Washington University. His writings include the books *Libraries, the First Amendment, and Cyberspace* and *The Bill of Rights and the Politics of Interpretation.* In the following selection he provides an overview of the evolution of Supreme Court decisions in free speech cases involving advocacy of violence. Early in the nation's history, such speech was viewed by legal authorities as being equivalent to violent actions that could be punished by law. The Supreme Court and other courts applied the "bad-tendency test"—the idea, found in English common law, that certain types of speech could be legally banned if they created a bad tendency toward unlawful acts. Over the course of the twentieth century, however, the Supreme Court moved away from the bad-tendency test and issued a series of rulings based on the theory that speech was protected as long as it did not incite or create immediate danger or harm—a principle some analysts have called the "clear and present danger test." By the 1970s the principle that the First Amendment protects even advocacy of violent acts was firmly established.

A familiar playground retort declares, "Sticks and stones may break my bones but names will never hurt me." The saying unintentionally captures an essential distinction

made in the law of free speech: The law properly concerns itself with punishing violent actions rather than mere violent
expression—or even the advocacy of violence.

Sedition and Slavery

Concern that some speech might give rise to violence is as
old as the Republic. In 1798, the Federalist Congress enacted
the Sedition Act, which made it a crime to "write, print, utter
or publish" or willingly assist in such expression, "any false,
scandalous and malicious writing or writings" against the
government, the Congress or the president. Federalist prosecutors and judges used the law to harass and arrest the Republican opposition. Supporters justified the act as necessary
to prevent inciting the people into sedition against their government. The act stirred up a great public discussion about
the importance of free speech and expired the day before Republican Thomas Jefferson became president.

If lessons were learned about the way in which a rationale built on prevention of violence could be enlisted to limit
political speech, the learning was short-lived. Soon, the issue
of slavery dominated the political debates. Abolitionists enlisted the enormous rhetorical power in denouncing that institution. They utilized the then-available forms of mass
communication, newspapers and tracts, and distributed
them widely in all slaveholding areas. Their efforts begat violence, as supporters of slavery burned abolitionist publications, broke up abolitionist meetings and beat up attendees,
and killed more than a few abolitionists in outbursts of mob
violence. Those seeking to suppress abolitionism heaped
blame on it for inciting such violence and stirring up the sup-
posedly otherwise docile slaves.

The accusations that abolitionism was a form of violent
incitement had impact. The postmaster general encouraged
his employees to withhold abolitionist publications, even
though he admitted he had no legal authority to do so. Another important incident took place in 1857 when Hinton
Rowan Helper authored a book attacking slavery, *The Im-
pending Crisis of the South: How to Meet It*. In slavery states,
those who endorsed or circulated the book were regarded as

felons. In at least one instance, a state sought their extradition to bring them to justice. After John Brown's violent raid on Harper's Ferry, slavery proponents charged that the book served as the percussion cap to that explosion. The speech, it was said, produced a bad tendency, which was sufficient to take it outside constitutional protection.

The Republican Party, which had adopted an antislavery platform and whose members had frequently endorsed the book, found itself accused of encouraging murder and arson. In response, it adopted the slogan, "free speech, free men, free territory, free soil." Once again, in the midst of a consuming controversy, the nation experienced a widespread debate on free speech that focused on its power to move people to violence.

Still, the idea of free speech remained but an abstract notion and lacked any pronouncement from the Supreme Court on the extent of its meaning or limitations. It may seem surprising that the First Amendment's guarantee of free speech, added to the Constitution as part of the Bill of Rights in 1791, did not figure in the Supreme Court's jurisprudence for more than a century. It was not until the 20th century that the Court waded into the meaning of this fundamental right—largely, in its early efforts, over the issue of incitement of violence.

The War Cases

World War I provided the occasion for the first judicial tests of free-speech rights. American involvement in the war brought significant protests, while others saw the Bolshevik revolution in Russia as a warning about an uprising from the left. Congress responded with the Espionage Act of 1917, criminalizing "false reports or false statements with intent to interfere" with military matters or promote the enemies' success, as well as interference with the recruitment and enlistment effort. A new Sedition Act in 1918 punished individuals who uttered, printed, wrote or published "Any disloyal, profane, scurrilous, or abusive language," intended to heap contempt upon government, the Constitution or the flag, as well as efforts deemed harmful to the war effort.

The Supreme Court upheld these laws. In *Schenck v. United States* (1919), the Court upheld the conviction of an individual who had mailed leaflets that argued that the military draft violated the 13th Amendment as a form of involuntary servitude and advocated repealing the draft law. Even though the leaflet was not accused of causing any instances of draft resistance, the Court found that its intention to bring about obstruction of the draft was clear. Justice Oliver Wendell Holmes Jr., writing for the Court, then famously declared: "The most stringent protection of free speech would not protect a man in falsely shouting fire in a theatre, and causing a panic."

One week later, the Court upheld two more decisions under the Espionage Act. In *Frohwerk v. United States* (1919), two individuals found guilty had published a newspaper in German that was critical of the U.S. war objectives. The efficacy of their effort was not an issue. It was enough, Justice Holmes wrote, that their writings could "kindle a flame" that could undermine the government's efforts. In *Debs v. United States* (1919), Socialist Party leader Eugene Debs was sentenced to 10 years in prison for declaring, in the midst of a speech on socialism, that "you need to know that you are fit for something better than slavery and cannon fodder," a reference to the military draft. That small statement was sufficient to run afoul of the Espionage Act's prohibition against interference with military recruitment.

In *Schenck*, Holmes had used the words "clear and present danger" to justify upholding the conviction. He soon received an opportunity to elaborate on what became known as the "clear and present danger" test, although this time it was in a dissent. Again, the vehicle for the Court's decision was a conviction under the Espionage Act. This time, the convicted individuals were Russian immigrants who had passed out leaflets to protest the dispatch of American troops to Eastern Europe after the Russian revolution. The Court, harking back to the idea that speech with the bad tendency to bring about harmful results, upheld the convictions in *Abrams v. United States* (1919).

Holmes dissented. He wrote that the government could only "punish speech that produces or is intended to produce a clear and imminent danger that it will bring about forthwith certain substantive evils." He added that "Congress certainly cannot forbid all effort to change the mind of the country." Instead, it is limited to regulating expressions that "so imminently threaten immediate interference with the lawful and pressing purposes of the law that an immediate check is required to save the country." That, he said, was not present in this case, which he characterized as involving "the surreptitious publishing of a silly leaflet by an unknown man."

The battle for supremacy between the bad-tendency test and the clear-and-present-danger test continued, as the Court sorted out which test best served constitutional purposes. In *Gitlow v. New York* (1925), the defendants had published a manifesto advocating political strikes and were convicted of a New York law that prohibited advocacy of the violent overthrow of the government. In upholding the convictions, the Court refused to use the clear and present analysis. In dissent, Holmes suggested that there was no real immediate danger and thus the First Amendment protected the speech in question.

Whitney v. California (1927) marked the last hurrah for the bad-tendency test. There, the Court upheld the conviction of a woman who had attended an organizational meeting of the California branch of the Communist Labor Party. Though she had taken a more mainstream position at the meeting than the others who had prevailed, the Court found that the legislature had the right to enact laws punishing her participation as an abuse of free speech because it determined it was "inimical to the public welfare, tend[ed] to incite to crime, disturb[ed] the public peace, or endanger[ed] the foundations of organized government and threaten[ed] its overthrow by unlawful means."

Justice Louis Brandeis, joined by Justice Holmes, concurred in an opinion that read more like a dissent. He wrote:

Fear of serious injury cannot alone justify suppression of free speech and assembly. Men feared witches and burnt women. It is the function of speech to free men from the bondage of irrational fears. To justify suppression of free speech there must be reasonable ground to fear that serious evil will result if free speech is practiced. There must be reasonable ground to believe that the danger apprehended is imminent. There must be reasonable ground to believe that the evil to be prevented is a serious one.

He added, "even advocacy of [law] violation however reprehensible morally, is not a justification for denying free speech where the advocacy falls short of incitement and there is nothing to indicate that the advocacy would be immediately acted upon."

The Communist Cases

The view expressed by Brandeis eventually prevailed as the modern approach to advocacy of violence. Still, the hysteria over communism that swept the country during the late 1940s and early 1950s affected the manner in which the clear-and-present-danger test, which had now prevailed, was applied. In *Dennis v. United States* (1951) the Court upheld the convictions under the 1940 Smith Act, which prohibited any person from advocating, abetting, advising or teaching the "duty, necessity, desirability, or propriety of overthrowing or destroying any government in the United States by force or violence." Their crime: teaching from four books written by Josef Stalin, Karl Marx and Frederic Engels, and Vladimir Lenin. In finding the convictions constitutional, the Court emphasized that imminence was not critical; it was enough that the actions had a probability of causing destruction of our governmental system, in the "context of world crisis after crisis."

In dissent, Justice William O. Douglas adhered to the need for a "present" danger of great imminency. He called it a "mystery" that the majority worried about some probability of success from a mere discussion of communist ideas, for the communists, he wrote, were merely "miserable merchants of unwanted ideas; their wares remain unsold."

When the issue returned to the Court a few years later, the Douglas view appeared to prevail, though the Court split hairs to leave the *Dennis* opinion intact. In *Yates v. United States* (1957) the Court overturned the convictions of U.S. Communist Party officials under the Smith Act by finding that the trial court had misconstrued the *Dennis* decision as obliterating "the traditional dividing line between advocacy of abstract doctrine and advocacy of action." Here, the Court moved closer to the Holmes understanding of the clear and present danger test as expressed in his dissent in *Abrams*.

Rallies, Protests, and Demonstrations

The denouement came in *Brandenburg v. Ohio* (1969). The case arose when a small group of Ku Klux Klan members in Ohio invited a television news station to film their rally. The handful of KKK members in attendance brandished rifles and firearms, made racist and anti-Semitic statements, and declared that they were going to march on Congress. The leader of the group was arrested and convicted under Ohio's version of the California law that had been used in the 1927 *Whitney* case. The Court overruled *Whitney*, declaring that subsequent decisions, including inexplicably *Dennis*, "have fashioned the principle that the constitutional guarantees of free speech and free press do not permit a State to forbid or regulate advocacy of the use of force or of law violation except where such advocacy is directed to inciting or producing imminent lawless action and is likely to incite or produce such action."

The case gave rise to the *Brandenburg* test to determine when speech transgresses the line from mere advocacy, which is protected by the First Amendment, to incitement, which is not. That test anticipates that the unprotected speech intentionally produce a high likelihood of real imminent harm. Within a few years, the Court had the opportunity to put that analysis to its own test.

Hess v. Indiana (1973) involved a student antiwar demonstration that had gotten out of hand and resulted in the police being called in riot gear. One student was arrested after he shouted, "We'll take the . . . street later." The Court was convinced that there was no imminent danger and interpreted his remark as advising students to stand down for now, with a suggestion that the illegal action of occupying the street could be resumed later. In the final analysis, the Court concluded that there was no evidence that "his words were intended to produce, and likely to produce, imminent disorder."

Soon, in *NAACP v. Claiborne Hardware Co.* (1982), the Court revisited the issue. The NAACP, as part of its civil rights efforts, had organized a boycott of white-owned businesses in Claiborne County, Miss., that allegedly discriminated against African-Americans. During the organization of the boycott, one NAACP official had said, "If we catch any of you going in any of them racist stores, we're gonna break your damn neck." Several businesses sued the NAACP for business losses incurred as a result of the boycott, specifically citing the NAACP's threat of violence against customers. A Mississippi court awarded the businesses $1.25 million.

Applying the *Brandenburg* test, the U.S. Supreme Court unanimously reversed. The First Amendment, the Court declared, does not permit the imposition of liability for nonviolent speech activities, but only for the consequences of violent conduct. Nor could liability be imposed on a group, some of whose members committed acts of violence, merely because of association with that group, which itself possessed only lawful goals, the Court added. Advocacy of imminent violent actions was first required.

The Court recognized that in "the passionate atmosphere in which the speeches were delivered, they might have been understood as inviting an unlawful form of discipline or, at least, intending to create a fear of violence where or not improper discipline was specifically intended." Still, "mere advocacy of the use of force or violence does not remove speech from the protection of the First Amendment."

That statement remains the bottom line on how the First Amendment views mere advocacy of violence. Today, when advocacy groups and some parents point the finger of blame on media depictions of violence on television and in lyrics, videogames, movies, and books, the law takes another view. As long as there is time for cooler heads to counter speech we find reprehensible or even dangerous, as long as the moment is not so enveloped in passion that deliberation cannot take place, each person is responsible for his or her own actions and the speaker-advocate cannot be hung with responsibility for their conduct. Experience has taught that grave dangers accompany any other course.

The First Amendment Does Not Protect Subversive Speech

Edward T. Sanford

In 1921 Benjamin Gitlow, a radical Socialist, was convicted of violating New York's Criminal Anarchy Act for publishing a tract that called for mass strikes and revolutionary actions to establish a Communist regime in the United States. On appeal to the Supreme Court, he argued that the conviction violated his free speech rights. A divided Supreme Court upheld his conviction in 1925 in *Gitlow v. New York*; excerpts from the majority opinion written by associate justice Edward T. Sanford are presented here. The Court argued that political dissent could be outlawed if, in the judgment of state legislators and other government officials, such dissent could possibly threaten the government—even if there was no proven imminent danger to the government or public order.

The case is historically significant because it marked the first time that justices agreed that freedom of speech is among the personal rights protected by the due process clause of the Fourteenth Amendment. Therefore, states— not just the federal government—must adhere to the First Amendment. This decision reversed a statement from a 1922 case (*Prudential Ins. Co. v. Cheek*) in which the Court ruled that states did not have the obligation to protect free speech. The Supreme Court in *Gitlow* did not provide any reasoning or argument about their historic change of position, which opened the door to future First Amendment challenges. Since *Gitlow* the majority of the Supreme Court's free speech decisions have involved state rather than federal actions.

Edward T. Sanford, majority opinion, *Gitlow v. New York*, 268 U.S. 652, 1925.

Benjamin Gitlow was indicted in the Supreme Court of New York, with three others, for the statutory crime of criminal anarchy. . . . He was separately tried, convicted, and sentenced to imprisonment. The judgment was affirmed by the Appellate Division and by the Court of Appeals. . . .

The contention here is that the statute, by its terms and as applied in this case, is repugnant to the due process clause of the Fourteenth Amendment. Its material provisions are:

> Section 160. *Criminal anarchy defined.* Criminal anarchy is the doctrine that organized government should be overthrown by force or violence, or by assassination of the executive head or of any of the executive officials of government, or by any unlawful means. The advocacy of such doctrine either by word of mouth or writing is a felony.
>
> Section 161. *Advocacy of criminal anarchy.* Any person who:
>
> 1. By word of mouth or writing advocates, advises, or teaches the duty, necessity, or propriety of overthrowing or overturning organized government by force or violence, or by assassination of the executive head or of any of the executive officials of government, or by any unlawful means; or,
>
> 2. Prints, publishes, edits, issues, or knowingly circulates, sells, distributes, or publicly displays any book, paper, document, or written or printed matter in any form containing or advocating, advising, or teaching the doctrine that organized government should be overthrown by force, violence, or any unlawful means . . . is guilty of a felony and punishable by imprisonment or fine, or both.

The indictment was in two counts. The first charged that the defendant had advocated, advised, and taught the duty, necessity, and propriety of overthrowing and overturning organized government by force, violence, and unlawful means, by certain writings therein set forth entitled "The Left Wing Manifesto"; the second, that he had printed, published, and knowingly circulated and distributed a certain paper called

The Revolutionary Age, containing the writings set forth in the first count advocating, advising, and teaching the doctrine that organized government should be overthrown by force, violence, and unlawful means. . . .

Effects of the Manifesto

There was no evidence of any effect resulting from the publication and circulation of the Manifesto. No witnesses were offered in behalf of the defendant. . . .

The sole contention here is, essentially, that as there was no evidence of any concrete result flowing from the publication of the Manifesto or of circumstances showing the likelihood of such result, the statute as construed and applied by the trial court penalizes the mere utterance, as such, of "doctrine" having no quality of incitement, without regard either to the circumstances of its utterance or to the likelihood of unlawful sequences; and that, as the exercise of the right of free expression with relation to government is only punishable "in circumstances involving likelihood of substantive evil," the statute contravenes the due process clause of the Fourteenth Amendment. The argument in support of this contention rests primarily upon the following propositions: 1st, that the "liberty" protected by the Fourteenth Amendment includes the liberty of speech and of the press; and 2d, that while liberty of expression "is not absolute," it may be restrained "only in circumstances where its exercise bears a causal relation with some substantive evil, consummated, attempted or likely," and as the statute "takes no account of circumstances," it unduly restrains this liberty and is therefore unconstitutional.

The precise question presented . . . is, whether the statute, as construed and applied in this case, by the State courts, deprived the defendant of his liberty of expression in violation of the due process clause of the Fourteenth Amendment.

The statute does not penalize the utterance or publication of abstract "doctrine" or academic discussion having no quality of incitement to any concrete action. It is not aimed against mere historical or philosophical essays. It does not restrain the advocacy of changes in the form of government by constitutional and lawful means. What it prohibits is language advocating, advising, or teaching the overthrow of organized government by unlawful means. These words imply urging to action. . . .

The Manifesto, plainly, is neither the statement of abstract doctrine nor, as suggested by counsel, mere prediction that industrial disturbances and revolutionary mass strikes will result spontaneously in an inevitable process of evolution in the economic system. It advocates and urges in fervent language mass action which shall progressively foment industrial disturbances and through political mass strikes and revolutionary mass action overthrow and destroy organized parliamentary government. It concludes with a call to action in these words:

> The proletariat revolution and the Communist reconstruction of society—the struggle for these—is now indispensable. . . . The Communist International calls the proletariat of the world to the final struggle!

This is not the expression of philosophical abstraction, the mere prediction of future events; it is the language of direct incitement.

The means, advocated for bringing about the destruction of organized parliamentary government, namely, mass industrial revolts usurping the functions of municipal government, political mass strikes directed against the parliamentary state, and revolutionary mass action fur its final destruction, necessarily imply the use of force and violence, and in their essential nature are inherently unlawful in a constitutional government of law and order. That the jury were warranted in finding that the Manifesto advocated not merely the abstract doctrine of overthrowing organized government by force, violence, and unlawful means, but action to that end, is clear.

Free Speech Not an Absolute Right

For present purposes we may and do assume that freedom of speech and of the press—which are protected by the First Amendment from abridgment by Congress—are among the fundamental personal rights and "liberties" protected by the due process clause of the Fourteenth Amendment from impairment by the States. We do not regard the incidental statement in *Prudential Ins. Co. v. Cheek*, that the Fourteenth Amendment imposes no restrictions on the States concerning freedom of speech, as determinative of this question.

It is a fundamental principle, long established, that the freedom of speech and of the press which is secured by the Constitution does not confer an absolute right to speak or publish, without responsibility, whatever one may choose, or an unrestricted and unbridled license that gives immunity for every possible use of language and prevents the punishment of those who abuse this freedom. . . .

That a State in the exercise of its police power may punish those who abuse this freedom by utterances inimical to the public welfare, tending to corrupt public morals, incite to crime, or disturb the public peace, is not open to question. . . .

And, for yet more imperative reasons, a State may punish utterances endangering the foundations of organized government and threatening its overthrow by unlawful means. These imperil its own existence as a constitutional State. Freedom of speech and press . . . does not protect disturbances to the public peace or the attempt to subvert the government. . . . It does not protect publications or teachings which tend to subvert or imperil the government or to impede or hinder it in the performance of its governmental duties. It does not protect publications prompting the overthrow of government by force; the punishment of those who publish articles which tend to destroy organized society being essential to the security of freedom and the stability of the State. . . . And a State may penalize utterances which openly advocate the overthrow of the representative and constitutional form of government of the United States and the several States, by violence or other unlawful means. . . . In short this freedom does not deprive a State of the primary and essential right of self preservation; which, so long as human governments endure, they cannot be denied. . . .

The Danger of a Revolutionary Spark

By enacting the present statute the State has determined, through its legislative body, that utterances advocating the overthrow of organized government by force, violence, and unlawful means, are so inimical to the general welfare and involve such danger of substantive evil that they may be penalized in the exercise of its police power. That determination must be given great weight. Every presumption is to be indulged in favor of the validity of the statute. . . . That utterances inciting to the overthrow of organized government by unlawful means, present a sufficient danger of substantive evil to bring their punishment within the range of legislative discretion, is clear. Such utterances, by their very nature, involve danger to the public peace and to the security of the State. They threaten breaches of the peace and ultimate revolution. And the immediate danger is none the less real and substantial, because the effect of a given utterance cannot be accurately foreseen. The State cannot reasonably be required to measure the danger from every such utterance in the nice balance of a jeweler's scale. A single revolutionary spark may kindle a fire that, smoldering for a time, may burst into a sweeping and destructive conflagration. It cannot be said that the State is acting arbitrarily or unreasonably when in the exercise of its judgment as to the measures necessary to protect the public peace and safety, it seeks to extinguish the spark without waiting until it has enkindled the flame or blazed into the conflagration. It cannot reasonably be required to defer the adoption of measures for its own peace and safety until the revolutionary utterances lead to actual disturbances of the public peace or imminent and immediate danger of its own destruction; but it may, in the exercise of its judgment, suppress the threatened danger in its incipiency. . . .

We cannot hold that the present statute is an arbitrary or unreasonable exercise of the police power of the State unwarrantably infringing the freedom of speech or press; and we must and do sustain its constitutionality.

This being so it may be applied to every utterance . . . which is of such a character and used with such intent and purpose as to bring it within the prohibition of the statute. . . . In other words, when the legislative body has determined generally, in the constitutional exercise of its discretion, that utterances of a certain kind involve such danger of substantive evil that they may be punished, the question whether any specific utterance coming within the prohibited class is likely, in and of itself, to bring about the substantive evil, is not open to consideration. It is sufficient that the statute itself be constitutional and that the use of the language comes within its prohibition. . . .

The Clear and Present Danger Test

The general statement in the *Schenck*[1] case, that the "question in every case is whether the words used are used in such circumstances and are of such a nature as to create a clear and present danger that they will bring about the substantive evils"—upon which great reliance is placed in the defendant's argument . . . has no application to [cases] like the present, where the legislative body itself has previously determined the danger of substantive evil arising from utterances of a specified character. . . . It was not necessary, within the meaning of the statute, that the defendant should have advocated "some definite or immediate act or acts" of force, violence, or unlawfulness. It was sufficient if such acts were advocated in general terms; and it was not essential that their immediate execution should have been advocated. Nor was it necessary that the language should have been "reasonably and ordinarily calculated to incite certain persons" to acts of force, violence, or unlawfulness. The advocacy need not be addressed to specific persons. Thus, the publication and circulation of a newspaper article may be an encouragement or endeavor to persuade to murder, although not addressed to any person in particular.

1. *Schenck v. United States*, 1919

Free Speech Should Be Restricted Only in Cases of Clear and Present Danger

Louis Brandeis

In 1927 the Supreme Court upheld the conviction of Anita Whitney under a California law that criminalized participation in an organization committed to violent means of effecting change in government (Whitney was a founding member of California's Communist Labor Party). *Whitney v. California* was the sixth case since 1919 in which the Supreme Court upheld the convictions of people convicted under federal or state sedition laws based on the principle that certain types of seditious speech had the "bad tendency" to produce illegal actions and/or threaten the government. The following selection is from the concurring opinion of Justice Louis Brandeis, who upheld Whitney's conviction on technical grounds but objected to the "bad tendency" arguments of the Supreme Court's majority. Expounding on ideas originated by fellow Supreme Court justice Oliver W. Holmes and Harvard Law School professor Zechariah Chaffee, Brandeis proposes an alternative way of interpreting the First Amendment in which speech would not be restricted unless it created a danger both "serious" and "imminent"—also known as the clear and present danger test. Brandeis also explains why free speech should be considered a fundamental right, arguing that speech is a vital means of personal self-fulfillment as well as an important tool of democracy. His opinion has been lauded by many as one of the most eloquent defenses of free speech written by a Supreme Court justice. Brandeis served on the Supreme Court from 1916 to 1939.

Louis Brandeis, opinion, *Whitney v. California*, 274 U.S. 357, 1927.

Miss Whitney was convicted of the felony of assisting in organizing, in the year 1919, the Communist Labor Party of California, of being a member of it, and of assembling with it. These acts are held to constitute a crime, because the party was formed to teach criminal syndicalism. The statute which made these acts a crime restricted the right of free speech and of assembly theretofore existing. The claim is that the statute, as applied, denied to Miss Whitney the liberty guaranteed by the Fourteenth Amendment.

The felony which the statute created is a crime very unlike the old felony of conspiracy or the old misdemeanor of unlawful assembly. The mere act of assisting in forming a society for teaching syndicalism, of becoming a member of it, or assembling with others for that purpose is given the dynamic quality of crime. There is guilt although the society may not contemplate immediate promulgation of the doctrine. Thus the accused is to be punished, not for attempt, incitement or conspiracy, but for a step in preparation, which, if it threatens the public order at all, does so only remotely. The novelty in the prohibition introduced is that the statute aims, not at the practice of criminal syndicalism, nor even directly at the preaching of it, but at association with those who propose to preach it.

Despite arguments to the contrary which had seemed to me persuasive, it is settled that the due process clause of the Fourteenth Amendment applies to matters of substantive law as well as to matters of procedure. Thus all fundamental rights comprised within the term liberty are protected by the federal Constitution from invasion by the states. The right of free speech, the right to teach and the right of assembly are, of course, fundamental rights. . . . These may not be denied or abridged. But, although the rights of free speech and assembly are fundamental, they are not in their nature absolute. Their exercise is subject to restriction, if the particular restriction proposed is required in order to protect the state from destruction or from serious injury, political, economic or moral. That the necessity which is essential to a valid restriction does not exist unless speech would produce, or is intended to produce, a clear and imminent danger of some substantive evil which the state constitutionally may seek to prevent has been settled. . . . It is said to be the function of the Legislature to determine whether at a particular time and under the particular circumstances the formation of, or assembly with, a society organized to advocate criminal syndicalism constitutes a clear and present danger of substantive evil; and that by enacting the law here in question the Legislature of California determined that question in the affirmative. . . . The Legislature must obviously decide, in the first instance, whether a danger exists which calls for a particular protective measure. But where a statute is valid only in case certain condition exist, the enactment of the statute cannot alone establish the facts which are essential to its validity. Prohibitory legislation has repeatedly been held invalid, because unnecessary, where the denial of liberty involved was that of engaging in a particular business. The powers of the courts to strike down an offending law are no less when the interests involved are not property rights, but the fundamental personal rights of free speech and assembly.

Establishing a Danger Standard

This court has not yet fixed the standard by which to determine when a danger shall be deemed clear; how remote the danger may be and yet be deemed present; and what degree of evil shall be deemed sufficiently substantial to justify resort to abridgment of free speech and assembly as the means of protection. To reach sound conclusions on these matters, we must bear in mind why a state is, ordinarily, denied the power to prohibit dissemination of social, economic and political doctrine which a vast majority of its citizens believes to be false and fraught with evil consequence. Those who won our independence believed that the final end of the state was to make men free to develop their faculties, and that in its government the deliberative forces should prevail over the arbitrary. They valued liberty both as an end and as a means. They believed liberty to the secret of happiness and courage to be the secret of liberty. They believed that freedom to think as you will and to speak as you think are means indispensable to the discovery and spread of political truth; that without free speech and assembly discussion would be futile; that with them, discussion affords ordinarily adequate protection against the dissemination of noxious doctrine; that the greatest menace to freedom is an inert people; that public discussion is a political duty; and that this should be a fundamental principle of the American government. They recognized the risks to which all human institutions are subject. But they knew that order cannot be secured merely through fear of punishment for its infraction; that it is hazardous to discourage thought, hope and imagination; that fear breeds repression; that repression breeds hate; that hate menaces stable government; that the path of safety lies in the opportunity to discuss freely supposed grievances and proposed remedies; and that the fitting remedy for evil counsels is good ones. Believing in the power of reason as applied through public discussion, they eschewed silence coerced by law—the argument of force in its worst form. Recognizing the occasional tyrannies of governing majorities, they amended the Constitution so that free speech and assembly should be guaranteed.

Fear of serious injury cannot alone justify suppression of free speech and assembly. Men feared witches and burnt women. It is the function of speech to free men from the bondage of irrational fears. To justify suppression of free speech there must be reasonable ground to fear that serious evil will result if free speech is practiced. There must be reasonable ground to believe that the danger apprehended is imminent. There must be reasonable ground to believe that the evil to be prevented is a serious one. Every denunciation of existing law tends in some measure to increase the probability that there will be violation of it. Condonation of a breach enhances the probability. Expressions of approval add to the probability. Propagation of the criminal state of mind by teaching syndicalism increases it. Advocacy of lawbreaking heightens it still further. But even advocacy of violation, however reprehensible morally, is not a justification for denying free speech where the advocacy falls short of incitement and there is nothing to indicate that the advocacy would be immediately acted on. The wide difference between advocacy and incitement, between preparation and attempt, between assembling and conspiracy, must be borne in mind. In order to support a finding of clear and present danger it must be shown either that immediate serious violence was to be expected or was advocated, or that the past conduct furnished reason to believe that such advocacy was then contemplated. Those who won our independence by revolution were not cowards. They did not fear political change. They did not exalt order at the cost of liberty. To courageous, self-reliant men, with confidence in the power of free and fearless reasoning applied through the processes of popular government, no danger flowing from speech can be deemed clear and present, unless the incidence of the evil apprehended is so imminent that it may befall before there is opportunity for full discussion. If there be time to expose through discussion the falsehood and fallacies, to avert the evil by the processes of education, the remedy to be applied is more speech, not enforced silence. Only an emergency can justify repression. Such must be the rule if authority is to be reconciled with freedom. Such, in my opinion, is the command of the Constitution. It is therefore always open to Americans to challenge a law abridging free speech and assembly by showing that there was no emergency justifying it.

Potential Harm Must Be Serious

Moreover, even imminent danger cannot justify resort to prohibition of these functions essential to effective democracy, unless the evil apprehended is relatively serious. Prohibition of free speech and assembly is a measure so stringent that it would be inappropriate as the means for averting a relatively trivial harm to society. . . . The fact that speech is likely to result in some violence or in destruction of property is not enough to justify its suppression. There must be the probability of serious injury to the State. Among free men, the deterrents ordinarily to be applied to prevent crime are education and punishment for violations of the law, not abridgment of the rights of free speech and assembly.

Arguing Hate Crime Laws and Free Speech Before the Supreme Court

Peter Irons

Early twentieth-century Supreme Court decisions on the First Amendment focused on state and federal laws aimed at Communists, anarchists, and other radicals. In the 1992 case of *RAV v. St. Paul*, the Supreme Court for the first time addressed the constitutionality of hate crime laws. Such laws, which were passed by many states and cities in the 1980s and 1990s, sought to punish expressions of animosity toward certain groups, typically by allowing extra punishment for acts committed against a person or person's property because of that person's race, gender, religion, nationality, sexual orientation, or other group characteristic. In 1990 a white teenager was convicted under a St. Paul, Minnesota, ordinance after he burned a cross on a black family's lawn. He challenged his conviction on free speech grounds. In 1992 the Supreme Court ruled in the case of *RAV v. Minnesota* that the city ordinance against "bias-motivated crime" violated the First Amendment. Many civil libertarians celebrated the decision as a victory for free speech. For example, the liberal *New Republic* magazine argued that the Supreme Court "has not only reaffirmed but dramatically extended the principle that government may not silence speech on the basis of its content, and that no insults, no matter how sharply they sting, may be singled out for punishment."

The following selection consists of excerpts from the oral arguments made before the Supreme Court on December 4, 1991, for the case of *RAV v. Minnesota*. It includes the

Peter Irons, ed., *May It Please the Court: The First Amendment*. New York: New Press, 1997.

presentations by the participating counsels—Ramsey county attorney Tom Foley and defense lawyer Edward J. Cleary— as well as their responses to questions from Supreme Court members. The transcript of the arguments was edited by political science professor Peter Irons, who also wrote the "Narrator" sections setting the scene for the arguments.

---

*C*ounsel for petitioner: Edward J. Cleary, St. Paul, Minnesota

Counsel for respondent: Tom Foley, Ramsey County Attorney, St. Paul, Minnesota

Chief Justice Rehnquist: We'll hear argument now in 90-7675, *R.A.V. v. St. Paul, Minnesota.*

Narrator: It's December 4, 1991. We're in the chamber of the United States Supreme Court in Washington, D.C. Chief Justice William Rehnquist has called for argument a case that tests the outer limits of the First Amendment.

This case began at 290 Earl Street in St. Paul, Minnesota. Early in 1990, Russell and Laura Jones and their five children moved into the working-class neighborhood of Dayton's Bluff. The Jones' were black and most of their neighbors were white. In the early morning of June 21, 1990, the Jones' heard noises, went outside and discovered a burning cross in their front yard. It was crudely made from two wooden chair legs, wrapped in terry cloth. The Jones' were terrified and quickly called the police.

Within a few days, the police arrested two teenage boys, who both lived near the Jones' home. They were charged under a St. Paul ordinance, adopted in 1982, which made it a crime to place on any property any symbol, object, or words that might arouse, in the law's words, "anger, alarm or resentment in others on the basis of race, color, creed, or gender. . . ." The law specified burning crosses and Nazi swastikas as prohibited symbols.

The St. Paul ordinance was one of many legal efforts to punish "hate crimes" during the 1980s. Legal challenges to such laws faced the obstacle of a 1942 Supreme Court ruling, upholding the conviction of Walter Chaplinsky, who called a

New Hampshire policeman a "goddamn fascist" during a street-corner altercation. The *Chaplinsky* case set out a "fighting words" exception to the First Amendment's free speech clause. However, in 1969 the Supreme Court ruled that Clarence Brandenburg, a Ku Klux Klan leader in Ohio, could not be punished for advocating violence against blacks and Jews, without a showing of "imminent lawless action."

The *Chaplinsky* and *Brandenburg* cases form the legal backdrop for today's argument. One of the boys charged in the cross burning pleaded guilty under the "hate crime" law. A juvenile court judge assigned a St. Paul lawyer, Edward Cleary, to represent the other boy, identified by his initials as R.A.V. His full name was Robert A. Viktora. Cleary had little in common with his client, who adopted "skinhead" attire and admitted contact with racist groups. But Cleary believed the "hate crime" law violated the First Amendment, and he persuaded a state judge to strike down the law on free speech grounds. But the Minnesota Supreme Court reversed this decision, citing the *Chaplinsky* and *Brandenburg* cases for authority. The U.S. Supreme Court granted Cleary's petition for review, and Chief Justice Rehnquist welcomes him to the podium.

Rehnquist: Mr. Cleary.

Cleary: Mr. Chief Justice, and may it please the Court. Each generation must reaffirm the guarantee of the First Amendment with the hard cases. The framers understood the dangers of orthodoxy and standardized thought and chose liberty. We are once again faced with a case that will demonstrate whether or not there is room for the freedom for the thought that we hate, whether there is room for the eternal vigilance necessary for the opinions that we loathe.

The conduct in this case is reprehensible, is abhorrent, and is well known by now. I'm not here to defend the alleged conduct, but as Justice [Felix] Frankfurter said forty years ago, history has shown that the safeguards of liberty are generally forged in cases involving not very nice people. He might just as well have said, involving cases involving very ugly fact situations. I am here to discuss and to ask the Court to review the Minnesota Supreme Court's interpretation of a St. Paul ordinance.

The *Chaplinsky* and *Brandenburg* Cases

Narrator: Justice Sandra O'Connor quickly asks Cleary to address the *Chaplinsky* and *Brandenburg* cases. He takes a cautious approach in responding.

O'Connor: And in essence what the Minnesota Supreme Court appears to have said is, we interpret the law as reaching only those exceptions that the Supreme Court has recognized to the First Amendment—fighting words, for instance, out of our prior *Chaplinsky* case. Now, do you agree that that's what they've done?

Cleary: I agree that the court attempted to narrow the ordinance and in doing so cited *Chaplinsky* and *Brandenburg* to this court.

O'Connor: Right, and in essence they said what that statute means is what the Supreme Court has permitted in *Brandenburg* and *Chaplinsky*.

Cleary: They did cite those cases, Your Honor. I do believe, however, that the expansive language that was used shows a much broader reach than what this Court indicated in those cases.

O'Connor: So you would ask us to somehow overturn those older holdings.

Cleary: No, I don't believe it's necessary to do that, Your Honor, to get to the position that I'm requesting.

Narrator: Asking the justices to overturn earlier decisions is always risky. Another question allows Cleary to suggest a way around *Chaplinsky*.

Court: Mr. Cleary, isn't one of your complaints that the Minnesota statute as construed by the supreme court of Minnesota punishes only some fighting words and not others?

Cleary: It is, Your Honor. That is one of my positions, that in doing so, even though it is a subcategory, technically, of unprotected conduct, it is still picking out an opinion, a disfavored message, and making that clear through the state. It's a paternalistic idea, and the problem we have is that the government must not betray neutrality, and I believe it does, even when it picks out a subcategory.

Narrator: Cleary had shied away from asking the justices to overturn the *Chaplinsky* decision, which defined "fighting words" as "those which by their very utterance inflict injury" on others. Questions on this issue move Cleary to shift his position on *Chaplinsky*.

Court: With respect just to the words that injure, where would you draw the line on what is permissible?

Cleary: I believe, Your Honor, that the—I'll be very honest. I think that's a very hard line to draw, and I think that's perhaps the crux of this case to a certain degree, is the offensiveness idea and how—

Court: Is it hard enough so that in fact we have to say that that was simply a mistaken statement and disavow it and leave *Chaplinsky* with the fighting words category as alone subject to punishment?

Cleary: No, I don't believe so. I believe that the Court must draw the line in favor of the individual right of self-expression. I think that if the line—

Court: Well, I agree, but aren't you really coming to the point of saying that the *Chaplinsky* reference to words that injure was in fact, at least by today's standards, an erroneous reference and we should disavow *Chaplinsky* to that extent?

Cleary: I am.

Laws Cannot Discriminate

Narrator: Cleary argues that the First Amendment does not permit laws to discriminate between "good" and "bad" attitudes or viewpoints toward minorities and women.

Cleary: The debate in this case is not about the wisdom of eradicating intolerance, the debate is about the method of reaching that goal. I believe that the city council officials in this case and in other communities are very well meaning, and that's usually the case, but the problem is that I believe these type of laws cross the line from the Fourteenth Amendment duty of the state to not participate in any racist state action or any intolerant state action, in that sense, with the First Amendment right of self-expression, even if it be intolerant, provided it does not cross the line of illegal conduct itself. I believe the danger in a law like this is that it does pick out viewpoints, that it is viewpoint-discriminatory.

Narrator: Minnesota has a law that punishes "terroristic threats" against others. Cleary faces questions about applying such a law to his client.

Court: Could this conduct be punished by a narrowly drawn statute that proscribes threats that cause violence? Could that state a cause of action against your client?

Cleary: I believe it could.

Court: On these facts?

Cleary: I believe it could. I believe, I have never argued that—again, that the conduct alleged in this case could not be addressed by viewpoint-neutral laws, but this type of a law leaves open the possibility for viewpoint discrimination, and it opens up, again, the selective enforcement idea.

Narrator: Cleary reminds the justices that the First Amendment was designed to protect free speech against fear and hysteria.

Cleary: Certainly in this current time there is a great deal of fear, and the First Amendment—and as it is construed and as it is before this Court, has to face the environment that we find ourselves in as a nation. Justice Brandeis once said that fear breeds repression and repression breeds hate. I believe that this is the hour of danger for the First Amendment in that there are many groups that would like to encroach upon its principles with well-meaning intentions, but in doing so, they are still punishing the content of the communication and they are doing so in a discriminatory manner, and the government is betraying a neutral principle in the sense that they are allowing that to happen and they are partaking in that.

Narrator: The Court ruled in 1989 that flag-burning was protected by the First Amendment, in *Texas v. Johnson.* Chief Justice Rehnquist dissented in that case, but he asks Cleary how the decision applies to cross burning. Cleary cites other "symbolic speech" cases—allowing red flags and black armbands as protest symbols—in his reply.

Rehnquist: The Court's opinion in *Texas* against *Johnson* suggested that there couldn't be a fighting symbol at any rate, per se, did it not?

Cleary: That's correct, Chief Justice. I think that the Court's holding in *Texas v. Johnson* supports the petitioners' position in this case, and I also would point out that I do not think that the dissents are necessarily inconsistent with the petitioners' position on this law. I would say that is particularly true because of the fact that this Court put a great emphasis on the unique nature of the American flag and in doing so, I believe, acknowledged the *Stromberg* red flag of the thirties, the black armband in the sixties, in *Tinker*, and was mindful of the fact that once that door is opened, that it could lead to a ban on symbolic behavior in such a fashion that a great deal of expression would be prohibited.

Defending Hate Crime Laws

Narrator: Tom Foley is the county attorney in St. Paul. He defends the city's "hate crime" law, and endorses the *Chaplinsky* and *Brandenburg* rulings as precedent.

Foley: Mr. Chief Justice, and may it please the Court. The First Amendment was never intended to protect an individual who burns a cross in the middle of the night in the fenced yard of an African-American family's home. The city of St. Paul has the right to prohibit and prosecute such conduct. The ordinance at issue in this case has been interpreted by the Minnesota Supreme Court to prohibit only conduct that inflicts injury, tends to incite an immediate breach of the peace, or provokes imminent lawless action.

And unless this Court is willing to abandon its holdings in *Chaplinsky* and *Brandenburg*, holdings that it has upheld for the last fifty years, this ordinance must be upheld.

Narrator: Foley outlines his argument, and immediately runs into questions from Justice O'Connor,

Foley: In this oral argument I'm going to touch on four propositions. First is the purpose of the ordinance. Second, that the ordinance has been narrowly construed by the Minnesota Supreme Court only to apply to fighting words. Third, that the ordinance as construed is not overbroad or vague. And fourth, that the ordinance does not interfere with legitimate First Amendment rights.

O'Connor: Well, Mr. Foley, would you address the concern expressed by your opponent that that ordinance is limited to only fighting words that arouse anger, alarm, or resentment on the basis of race, color, creed, or religion or gender and not other fighting words that could cause the same reaction in people? The argument is that the statute is underinclusive.

Foley: Your Honor, it's our position that the statute is not underinclusive, that this is a fighting words case, that this is unprotected conduct under the First Amendment, and that the city of St. Paul has the right to determine which harms it can proscribe within the limits of its jurisdiction.

O'Connor: Well, certainly it is limited by subject matter or content of the fighting words that are spoken, is it not? In that sense it is a content-based ordinance.

Foley: Your Honor, it's our position that it is not a content-based ordinance, that it certainly could be used to be a content-neutral ordinance.

O'Connor: Well, but it doesn't cover fighting words that are not limited to words on the basis of race, color, creed, religion, or gender.

Foley: That's correct, Your Honor.

Questions from Justice Scalia

Narrator: Picking up where Justice O'Connor ended, Justice Scalia turns up the heat on Foley.

Scalia: If you want to prohibit fighting words, prohibit fighting words. But why pick only if you use fighting words for these particular purposes: race, color, creed, religion, and gender? What about other fighting words?

Foley: I think the city has an absolute right and purpose to try to regulate the harm that goes on to its citizens. And certainly this bias-motivated conduct and violence is much more harmful and has more harmful impacts to its citizens—

Scalia: That's a political judgment. I mean, you may feel strongest about race, color, creed, religion, or gender. Somebody else may feel strong as to about philosophy, about economic philosophy, about whatever. You picked out five reasons for causing somebody to breach the peace. But there are a lot of other ones. What's your basis for making that subjective discrimination?

Foley: Your Honor, the city of St. Paul is attempting to fashion responses to violence that it deems necessary to prohibit and will add additional harms to be regulated as it finds them. Under this particular ordinance, it seemed that this is a particular harm going on that is necessary within the city of St. Paul to prohibit and regulate.

Scalia: It doesn't have to add anything. You could just drop the words and, you know, just say that arouses anger, alarm, or resentment in others, period, or shall be guilty of a misdemeanor. It didn't have to say arouses anger, alarm, or resentment on the basis of race, color, creed, religion, or gender. You don't need that for *Chaplinsky.* If it's a fighting word, it's a fighting word. They could get the cross burning, they could get all sorts of activities.

Foley: Your Honor, I think it's the city's position that this is a fighting words case, that the ordinance has been sufficiently narrowed by the Minnesota Supreme Court. And you could reread that ordinance under these facts to say that whoever, based on race, places an object or symbol with the intent to inflict injury, incite immediate violence, or provoke imminent lawless action is guilty of a crime. And I think that the Minnesota Supreme Court's narrowing of that ordinance is sufficient to uphold its constitutionality under the *Chaplinsky* and *Brandenburg* holdings of this Court.

Scalia: Well, are you saying that because they can prevent or punish all fighting words, they can select any category within the broad scope of fighting words for it to be singled out?

Foley: Yes, Your Honor.

Narrator: Foley tries to move on, but his claim that St. Paul can pick and choose the groups to protect from hate crimes provokes another round of questions from Justice Scalia.

Foley: I think it is important to look at bias-motivated violence, which is significantly more harmful on the impact than similar criminal conduct not similarly motivated. The burning of the cross and the African-American family is not the equivalent of a simple trespass or minor arson, either to the targeted victims or to the community in which it occurred.

Scalia: Well, you say bias-motivated, but it depends on what your biases are. If a family with a mentally deficient child should move into the neighborhood or if there should be established in the neighborhood a home for the mentally ill, and someone should burn a cross on the lawn of that home or institution with a sign that says, mentally ill out, that would not be covered by this ordinance, isn't that correct?

Foley: I don't believe under the facts that you described that it would.

Scalia: It's the wrong kind of bias. It's—at least until they come around to adding—which may well be the next one, gender, religion, gender, or disability, until they come around to adding that, it's the wrong kind of bias and therefore you can't—

Foley: It's probably not addressed under this particular ordinance. There are other alternative criminal laws that may apply to that particular situation.

Scalia: Why is that? I mean, if you are concerned about breaches of the public peace, if it's a fighting words problem, why is it okay for the state to have the public peace broken for that reason? It's only these, other reasons they are worried about, why is that? That seems to me like the rankest kind of subject matter discrimination.

Foley: Well, there are many reasons that cities and state legislatures look to a particular wrong that they are attempting to address, and I don't think they address all of those wrongs at the same time, and they attempt to get as many of them as they can, and they do address in a content-based— under certain circumstances, certain harms that they want to address and including—

Scalia: It wasn't hard to write this in such a way that it wouldn't discriminate in that fashion. They just had to drop out, on the basis of race, color, creed, religion, or gender, but those are the only things that they seemed to be concerned about.

Foley: I think the Minnesota Supreme Court addressed or made reference to that issue when it said that the particular city ordinance could have been drawn a little bit better, but then went on to clearly narrow the impact of that ordinance and narrowed it only to apply to fighting words. And in the context of the facts of this case, the burning of the cross, the historical context of a burning cross in the middle of the night is a precursor to violence and hatred in this country.

Victims of Hate Crimes

Narrator: Foley concludes with a reminder of the impact of hate crimes on victims like the Jones family.

Foley: In the case of bias-motivated crimes, there is a compelling state purpose to deal with what is a cancer on society, and it will, unless effectively dealt with, spread throughout the community. Bias motivated crimes have a devastating effect on the particular target victims and equally profound effect on all members of the minority that is indirectly targeted and a pervasive effect on the community as a whole.

Given the historical experience of African-Americans, a burning cross targeted at a black family under the circumstances outlined is an unmistakable threat. Terroristic conduct such as this can find no protection in the Constitution. Thank you, Your Honors.

The Supreme Court's Decision

Narrator: On June 22, 1992—two years and one day after Robert Viktora burned a cross in the front yard of the Jones family—the Supreme Court ruled that St. Paul's "hate crimes" ordinance violated the First Amendment. The decision was unanimous, but the justices agreed on hardly anything in this hard case. The four separate opinions in *R.A.V. v. St. Paul* exposed the deep—almost bitter—divisions within the Court over the troubling issue of hate speech.

Justice Antonin Scalia had peppered both lawyers with questions during oral argument. He left no doubt that he considered the law an impermissible content-based regulation of speech, in his opinion for the Court, Scalia took a hard line. Singling out for punishment any category of speech, based on its viewpoint or message, violates the First Amendment. No matter how offensive the message may be, creating "favored" and "disfavored" categories of speech turns the government into a censorship board. "The First Amendment," Scalia wrote, "does not permit St. Paul to impose special prohibitions on those speakers who express views on disfavored subjects." Scalia spoke in his opinion for Chief Justice Rehnquist and Justices Anthony Kennedy, David Souter, and Clarence Thomas.

The remaining four justices agreed that the ordinance violated the First Amendment. However, as Justice Byron White wrote, "our agreement ends there." White accused Scalia of tossing out the "fighting words" exception to protected speech in the *Chaplinsky* case. This category of speech, White stated, "is by definition worthless and undeserving of constitutional protection." Had the St. Paul city council enacted a more narrowly-drawn law, Justice White would have upheld Robert Viktora's conviction. But the law was "overbroad" in banning all speech that might arouse anger or resentment. The vice of the law, White wrote, was that it reaches beyond "fighting words" and "criminalizes a substantial amount of expression that—however repugnant—is shielded by the First Amendment."

The Court's decision in *R.A.V.* leaves the "fighting words" doctrine in limbo. The justices have not upheld a conviction based on *Chaplinsky*, but they haven't overruled this historic decision, preferring to leave it in their judicial arsenal. Back in St. Paul, the Court's decision changed very little. Robert Viktora got into trouble again, after a skinhead companion yelled "White Power" at a police officer. Viktora was fined $100 for scuffling with the officer. The Jones family still lives in their home on Earl Street, but there have been other cross burnings in the area. Racial tensions create a tinderbox in many American communities. The hard job, as Justice Scalia wrote, is to deal with these tensions "without adding the First Amendment to the fire."

CHAPTER THREE

Obscenity and Freedom of Expression

The Bill of Rights

The Supreme Court Defines Obscenity

Warren Burger

In the 1957 case of *Roth v. United States*, the Supreme Court affirmed the view that obscenity lacks First Amendment protection. The Court defined obscene speech as being "utterly without redeeming social importance" in which "to the average person, applying contemporary community standards, the dominant theme of the material taken as a whole appeals to prurient interest." However, for the next sixteen years the Supreme Court was unable to reach a definition of obscenity that satisfied a majority of its members. A new standard was finally established in the case of *Miller v. California*, decided in June 1973, which upheld the conviction of a man for violating a California obscenity law against sending a mass mailing advertisement featuring sexual pictures and drawings. Chief Justice Warren Burger, who was appointed by President Richard Nixon in 1969 and served as chief justice until 1986, wrote the deciding opinion, joined by four others. Burger established a three-part test to define obscenity as material that appealed to prurient interest, portrayed sexual conduct "in a patently offensive way," and did not have "serious literary, artistic, political, or scientific value." Excerpts from Burger's opinion are found in the following selection.

This is one of a group of "obscenity-pornography" cases being reviewed by the Court in a reexamination of standards enunciated in earlier cases involving what Mr. Justice Harlan called "the intractable obscenity problem." . . .

Warren Burger, opinion, *Miller v. California*, 413 U.S. 15, 1973.

Apart from the initial formulation in the *Roth* case, no majority of the Court has at any given time been able to agree on a standard to determine what constitutes obscene, pornographic material subject to regulation under the States' police power. . . .

This much has been categorically settled by the Court, that obscene material is unprotected by the First Amendment. . . . We acknowledge, however, the inherent dangers of undertaking to regulate any form of expression. State statutes designed to regulate obscene materials must be carefully limited. . . . As a result, we now confine the permissible scope of such regulation to works which depict or describe sexual conduct. That conduct must be specifically defined by the applicable state law, as written or authoritatively construed. A state offense must also be limited to works which, taken as a whole, appeal to the prurient interest in sex, which portray sexual conduct in a patently offensive way, and which, taken as a whole, do not have serious literary, artistic, political, or scientific value.

Basic Guidelines

The basic guidelines for the trier of fact must be: (a) whether "the average person, applying contemporary community standards" would find that the work, taken as a whole, appeals to the prurient interest . . . ; (b) whether the work depicts or describes, in a patently offensive way, sexual conduct specifically defined by the applicable state law; and (c) whether the work, taken as a whole, lacks serious literary, artistic, political, or scientific value. . . .

If a state law that regulates obscene material is thus limited, as written or construed, the First Amendment values applicable to the States through the Fourteenth Amendment are adequately protected by the ultimate power of appellate courts to conduct an independent review of constitutional claims when necessary. . . .

Sex and nudity may not be exploited without limit by films or pictures exhibited or sold in places of public accommodation any more than live sex and nudity can be exhibited or sold without limit in such public places. At a minimum, prurient, patently offensive depiction or description of sexual

conduct must have serious literary, artistic, political, or scientific value to merit First Amendment protection. . . .

It is certainly true that the absence, since *Roth*, of a single
majority view of this Court as to proper standards for testing
obscenity has placed a strain on both state and federal courts.
But today, for the first time since *Roth* was decided in 1957, a
majority of this Court has agreed on concrete guidelines to
isolate "hard core" pornography from expression protected by
the First Amendment. Now we may . . . attempt to provide
positive guidance to federal and state courts alike.

This may not be an easy road, free from difficulty. But no
amount of "fatigue" should lead us to adopt a convenient "in-
stitutional" rationale—an absolutist, "anything goes" view of
the First Amendment—because it will lighten our burdens.

No National Standard

Under a National Constitution, fundamental First Amendment limitations on the powers of the States do not vary from
community to community, but this does not mean that there
are, or should or can be, fixed, uniform national standards of
precisely what appeals to the "prurient interest" or is
"patently offensive." These are essentially questions of fact,
and our Nation is simply too big and too diverse for this
Court to reasonably expect that such standards could be articulated for all 50 States in a single formulation, even as-
suming the prerequisite consensus exists. When triers of fact
are asked to decide whether "the average person, applying
contemporary community standards" would consider certain
materials "prurient," it would be unrealistic to require that
the answer be based on some abstract formulation. The ad-
versary system, with lay jurors as the usual ultimate
factfinders in criminal prosecutions, has historically permitted triers of fact to draw on the standards of their community, guided always by limiting instructions on the law. To
require a State to structure obscenity proceedings around evidence of a national "community standard" would be an exercise in futility. . . .

It is neither realistic nor constitutionally sound to read the
First Amendment as requiring that the people of Maine or

Mississippi accept public depiction of conduct found tolerable in Las Vegas, or New York City. . . . People in different States vary in their tastes and attitudes, and this diversity is not to be strangled by the absolutism of imposed uniformity. . . .

The dissenting Justices sound the alarm of repression. But, in our view, to equate the free and robust exchange of ideas and political debate with commercial exploitation of obscene material demeans the grand conception of the First Amendment and its high purposes in the historic struggle for freedom. . . . The First Amendment protects works which, taken as a whole, have serious literary, artistic, political, or scientific value, regardless of whether the government or a majority of the people approve of the ideas these works represent. . . . But the public portrayal of hard-core sexual conduct for its own sake, and for the ensuing commercial gain, is a different matter. . . .

We do not see the harsh hand of censorship of ideas—good or bad, sound or unsound—and "repression" of political liberty lurking in every state regulation of commercial exploitation of human interest in sex. . . .

In sum, we (a) reaffirm the *Roth* holding that obscene material is not protected by the First Amendment; (b) hold that such material can be regulated by the States, subject to the specific safeguards enunciated above, without a showing that the material is "utterly without redeeming social value"; and (c) hold that obscenity is to be determined by applying "contemporary community standards" not "national standards."

There Should Be No Obscenity Exception to Free Speech

William O. Douglas

The Supreme Court in the 1973 case of *Miller v. California* reaffirmed its position that obscenity was not protected by the First Amendment and developed a test for defining obscenity. Justice William O. Douglas wrote a dissenting opinion, which is presented in the following selection. Arguing that obscenity is not mentioned in the First Amendment, nor in the entire Bill of Rights, he contends that obscenity should be protected to the same degree as other forms of speech. The First Amendment protects the right to speech others find offensive, he concludes. Douglas served on the Supreme Court from 1939 to 1975.

Today [June 21, 1973] the Court retreats from the earlier formulations of the constitutional test and undertakes to make new definitions. This effort, like the earlier ones, is earnest and well intentioned. The difficulty is that we do not deal with constitutional terms, since "obscenity" is not mentioned in the Constitution or Bill of Rights. And the First Amendment makes no such exception from "the press" which it undertakes to protect, nor, as I have said on other occasions, is an exception necessarily implied, for there was no recognized exception to the free press at the time the Bill of Rights was adopted which treated "obscene" publications differently from other types of papers, magazines, and books. So there are no constitutional guidelines for deciding what is and what is not "obscene." The Court is at large because we deal with tastes and standards of literature. What shocks me may be

William O. Douglas, dissenting opinion, *Miller v. California*, 413 U.S. 15, 1973.

sustenance for my neighbor. What causes one person to boil up in rage over one pamphlet or movie may reflect only his neurosis, not shared by others. We deal here with a regime of censorship which, if adopted, should be done by constitutional amendment after full debate by the people. . . .

The First Amendment Protects Offensive Speech

The idea that the First Amendment permits government to ban publications that are "offensive" to some people puts an ominous gloss on freedom of the press. That test would make it possible to ban any paper or any journal or magazine in some benighted place. The First Amendment was designed "to invite dispute," to induce "a condition of unrest," to "create dissatisfaction with conditions as they are," and even to stir "people to anger." *Terminiello v. Chicago* [1949]. The idea that the First Amendment permits punishment for ideas that are "offensive" to the particular judge or jury sitting in judgment is astounding. No greater leveler of speech or literature has ever been designed. To give the power to the censor, as we do today, is to make a sharp and radical break with the traditions of a free society. The First Amendment was not fashioned as a vehicle for dispensing tranquilizers to the people. Its prime function was to keep debate open to "offensive" as well as to "staid" people. The tendency throughout history has been to subdue the individual and to exalt the power of government. The use of the standard "offensive" gives authority to government that cuts the very vitals out of the First Amendment. As is intimated by the Court's opinion, the materials before us may be garbage. But so is much of what is said in political campaigns, in the daily press, on TV, or over the radio. By reason of the First Amendment—and solely because of it—speakers and publishers have not been threatened or subdued because their thoughts and ideas may be "offensive" to some. . . .

If there are to be restraints on what is obscene, then a constitutional amendment should be the way of achieving the end. There are societies where religion and mathematics are the only free segments. It would be a dark day for America if that were our destiny. But the people can make it such if they choose to write obscenity into the Constitution and define it.

Emotional Questions

We deal with highly emotional, not rational, questions. To many the Song of Solomon is obscene. I do not think we, the judges, were ever given the constitutional power to make definitions of obscenity. If it is to be defined, let the people debate and decide by a constitutional amendment what they want to ban as obscene and what standards they want the legislatures and the courts to apply. Perhaps the people will decide that the path towards a mature, integrated society requires that all ideas competing for acceptance must have no censor. Perhaps they will decide otherwise. Whatever the choice, the courts will have some guidelines. Now we have none except our own predilections.

Censoring Indecency on the Radio Threatens Free Speech

Jonathan D. Wallace

Jonathan D. Wallace, a lawyer and software company executive, is the coauthor of *Sex, Laws, and Cyberspace*. In the following selection, he examines the 1978 case of *Pacifica Foundation v. FCC*, in which the Supreme Court permitted the censorship of obscene words on radio broadcasts. Wallace describes the incident and lawsuit that led to the decision and the Supreme Court's reasoning that the "pervasiveness" of radio broadcast justified government censorship to protect children from obscene and offensive language. Wallace argues that the Supreme Court's reasoning in *Pacifica* could be used to justify censorship in other areas and may well threaten free speech on the Internet.

O n a Tuesday afternoon in October 1973, a motorist in the New York area tuned his radio to WBAI-FM and heard a 12-minute monologue by comedian George Carlin entitled "Filthy Words." The routine, included on Carlin's record *Occupation: Foole*, had been taped during a live performance in California. The topic was the "words you couldn't say on the public airwaves, the ones you definitely wouldn't say, ever." Carlin began by listing the seven words designated by the FCC as unacceptable for broadcast media. . . . "These are the ones that will curve your spine, grow hair on your hands, and maybe even bring us, God help us, peace without honor, and a bourbon." The driver who happened upon Carlin's monologue, later described in court records as accompanied by his "young son," wrote a letter of complaint to the Federal

Communications Commission. His was the only complaint received about the Carlin broadcast. Although the court records did not say so, the driver was a board member of Morality in Media who was visiting the New York area from his home in Florida, and his "young son" was 15 years old.

The FCC responded by placing a letter of sanction in its file for the Pacifica Foundation, which operated WBAI. Pacifica challenged the action on First Amendment grounds, and the case wended its way up to the Supreme Court, which issued a fragmentary and confusing decision in July 1978. Supporting the FCC's authority to regulate "indecent" speech on the airwaves, the Court emphasized that radio broadcasts "pervade" people's homes and may be heard by unattended children. It thereby introduced a new and controversial doctrine into American constitutional law: Government may regulate a communications medium because of its "pervasiveness."

Most commentators originally thought *Pacifica Foundation v. FCC*, destined to be known as "the seven dirty words case," applied only to broadcast media. But in his 1983 book *Technologies of Freedom*, communications scholar Ithiel de Sola Pool argued that the pervasiveness doctrine could be used to justify "quite radical censorship." He was right. In recent years, *Pacifica* has been cited by the Supreme Court in a case upholding restrictions on cable TV, and it was the foundation for the Communications Decency Act, which attempted to regulate speech on the Internet.

When the Supreme Court overturned the CDA in the 1997 case *ACLU v. Reno*, it did not reject the pervasiveness doctrine. Instead, it held that the Internet is not pervasive. But this finding was based on such narrow grounds that it is bound to be undermined by technological developments. Furthermore, if the logic of the pervasiveness doctrine were applied consistently, even the print media would not be safe from censorship. As long as *Pacifica* remains the law, defenders of free speech, online or off, cannot rest easy.

Pornography, Obscenity, and Indecency

To understand what happens when the government tries to protect us against "indecency" in "pervasive" media, it is important to recognize how broad that category of speech is. Although many people use the words *pornography, obscenity,* and *indecency* interchangeably, the law understands them very differently. *Pornography* is a popular term with no legal meaning. *Obscenity,* as defined by the Supreme Court in the 1973 case *Miller v. California,* is patently offensive, prurient material, lacking significant scientific, literary, artistic, or political ("SLAP") value. The *Miller* standard has been used almost exclusively against distributors of hardcore visual material—pictorial magazines and videos—that lack perceived SLAP value. *Indecency,* by contrast, is "patently offensive" material that may have significant SLAP value, and it need not include pictures. Historically, indecency laws in the United States were used to prosecute writers and publishers of controversial novels (including the works of Balzac, Tolstoy, Zola, and Joyce), along with early crusaders for women's sexual independence, abortion rights, and birth control.

The main justification for indecency laws has always been protecting children. The Supreme Court has repeatedly held that unlike obscenity, which is considered outside the scope of First Amendment protection, indecent material cannot be banned. It can only be "channeled"—regulated so that it is kept away from children. In *Butler v. Michigan,* a 1957 decision overturning a state ban on indecent literature, the Court said adults cannot be reduced to reading "only what is fit for children." Writing for the majority, Justice Felix Frankfurter said to ban indecency for the sake of children is "to burn the house to roast the pig."

The question in *Pacifica* was whether the restrictions on broadest indecency, like the ban at issue in *Butler,* impermissibly infringed on the freedom of adults. The Supreme Court was reassured by the fact that the FCC's regulations, unlike the Michigan law, did not carry criminal sanctions. The consequence of Pacifica's infraction was not a prison term or even a fine—just a letter of reprimand (which could, in theory, affect the FCC's willingness to renew the station's license). The Court's concerns were also allayed by the narrowness of the FCC's "seven dirty words" rule. The majority argued that speakers could always find another vocabulary to express the same ideas.

Shock Jocks

The broadcast industry took this statement as an invitation. The 1980s and '90s saw the proliferation of "shock jocks": loud, crude (and highly popular) radio hosts—typified by Howard Stern—who frequently found ways to talk about sex without using the seven dirty words. In response, the FCC broadened its definition of indecency to include suggestive language that didn't use any of the original seven dirty words. Beginning in 1986, indecency was defined as "patently offensive" language describing sexual or excretory acts or organs. In 1988 Congress tried to ban broadcast indecency entirely, but the Supreme Court, consistent with its ruling in *Butler*, said that approach went too far. Instead, the FCC continued to "channel" broadcast indecency by restricting it to the late evening and early morning (10 P.M. to 6 A.M.), when children were less likely to be listening or watching.

With the broader definition of indecency in place, listener complaints investigated by the FCC increasingly dealt with sexual insinuations. Infinity Broadcasting, the syndicator backing Howard Stern, was fined millions of dollars for some of his excesses, including a show featuring a man who played the piano with his penis (on the radio, remember) and Stern's comment that "the closest I ever came to making love to a black woman was masturbating to a picture of Aunt Jemima."

But speech need not be frivolous to be considered indecent. Flipping channels as a teenager, I came across a PBS documentary about breast cancer that ended with a brief sequence of a woman examining her breast. Nothing in the FCC's indecency regulations excludes the possibility that a television station could be sanctioned, or have its license renewal application denied, for broadcasting such a documentary. Broadcasters have to rely on the good sense and forbearance of FCC bureaucrats to protect socially valuable speech.

That is bound to have a chilling effect on programming, because broadcasters have to anticipate what the FCC will consider indecent, and even material with a serious point can run afoul of the rules. In 1989, for example, the FCC fined a Miami radio station for playing the Uncle Bonsai song "Penis Envy," a satire of macho attitudes. It has also found excerpts from the critically acclaimed play *Jerker*, in which two gay men discuss their sexual fantasies over the telephone, to be indecent. Social conservatives have even suggested FCC action against TV news coverage showing Madonna's "Justify My Love" video and sexually explicit photographs by Robert Mapplethorpe—both of which were aired precisely because they had been subjects of controversy.

Even the old definition of indecency went beyond gratuitous profanity. Carlin, after all, was making a political statement by mocking the very system of regulation that made it illegal to air his monologue. Justice William Brennan dissented from the *Pacifica* decision because its rationale "could justify the banning from radio of a myriad of literary works, novels, poems and plays by the likes of Shakespeare, Joyce, Hemingway." He noted that *Pacifica* would allow the suppression of political speech "such as the Nixon tapes" and could even result in sanctions for broadcasting portions of the Bible. In particular, he cited I Samuel 25:22, where King David threatens Nabal, a wealthy man who has treated his messengers rudely: "So and more also do God unto the enemies of David, if I leave of all that pertain to him by the morning light any that pisseth against the wall."

The Pervasiveness Doctrine

If the concept of indecency is disturbingly elastic, so is the idea of pervasiveness. The puzzling thing about the Supreme Court's invention of the pervasiveness doctrine in *Pacifica* is that it was not necessary to resolve the case. For half a century, the government's power to regulate broadcasting had been based on the idea of "spectrum scarcity": Since there are a limited number of frequencies available for broadcasting on "the public airwaves," the government must decide who gets to use them, and it may attach conditions to that privilege. Critics of this doctrine have long argued that it does not justify a lower level of First Amendment protection for broadcasting, since all media, including books and newspapers, use scarce resources. Yet the Court has repeatedly relied on the spectrum scarcity argument, and it could have done so again in *Pacifica*.

Instead, the Court declared that "the broadcast media have established a uniquely pervasive presence in the lives of all Americans. Patently offensive, indecent material presented over the airwaves confronts the citizen, not only in public, but also in the privacy of the home, where the individual's right to be left alone plainly outweighs the First Amendment rights of an intruder." For nearly two decades, no one really knew what to make of the pervasiveness doctrine. Was "pervasiveness" a feature only of a "scarce" medium, such as radio or television? Or could other media, such as cable TV and online services, be regulated as pervasive?

Two centuries of case law had finally established that any idea may be explored in print, no matter what language is used. Under those precedents, no law could ban the use of the seven dirty words in this article or in any publication, scholarly or frivolous. It might seem to be a matter of common sense that every medium would be granted the same protection. Why should technical distinctions be the basis for different treatment under the First Amendment? . . .

In the 1996 case *Denver Area Telecommunications Consortium v. FCC*, the Court ruled that cable television, though not "scarce," is "pervasive." The case involved a federal law requiring cable providers either to ban indecent programming or to block it, delivering it only to viewers who request it. Justice Stephen Breyer, writing for the plurality, approvingly summarized *Pacifica*'s finding that "the broadcast media have established a uniquely pervasive presence in the lives of all Americans" and that "patently offensive, indecent material . . . confronts the citizen, not only in public, but also in the privacy of the home." Such exposure, he said, was "generally without sufficient prior warning to allow the recipient to avert his or her eyes or ears." Several other justices relied on *Pacifica* in their concurring opinions. Only Justice Clarence Thomas took a clear stand against differentiating cable from print media. "The text of the First Amendment," he noted, "makes no distinction between print, broadcast, and cable media."

Commentators had long wondered why cable TV should be treated differently than broadcast TV, when the experience of watching them is essentially the same. Why should it matter, for First Amendment purposes, if the image is delivered to the house via the airwaves or over a cable? *Denver* seemed to give the Court's answer: It doesn't.

The Communications Decency Act

But this meant we were now facing the possibility of the "quite radical censorship" de Sola Pool had predicted. The next logical question was why it should matter if the same images or words are delivered to the house via the Internet. Congress did not think it should: With the Communications Decency Act of 1996, it applied the FCC's indecency standard to the Internet, establishing a penalty of up to two years in prison and a $100,000 fine for each violation. The law's proponents relied heavily on *Pacifica* and the pervasiveness argument to justify the legislation. Sen. Dan Coats (R-Ind.), one of the CDA's main sponsors, said during congressional debate in June 1995, "The Internet is like taking a porn shop and putting it in the bedroom of your children and then saying, 'Do not look.'" . . .

A special three-judge federal panel in Philadelphia conducted a trial on the law's constitutionality in the winter and spring of 1996. . . .

The three Philadelphia judges were unanimous in deciding that the CDA was unconstitutional and that the Internet was entitled to extensive First Amendment protection. Each wrote a separate concurring opinion. In the, Judge Stewart Dalzell addressed the question of whether *Pacifica* applied to the Internet. . . . He concluded that "time has not been kind to the *Pacifica* decision. Later cases have eroded its reach, and the Supreme Court has repeatedly instructed against overreading the rationale of its holding."

But in a footnote, Dalzell wisely offered a second, independent argument against applying *Pacifica* to the Internet: "Operation of a computer is not as simple as turning on a television, and the . . . assaultive nature of television . . . is quite absent in Internet use. . . . The Government may well be right that sexually explicit content is just a few clicks of a mouse

away from the user, but there is an immense legal signifi-
cance to those few clicks."

A year later, the Supreme Court agreed that the CDA was
unconstitutional—and that the Internet is not pervasive.
Quoting the Philadelphia opinions, the Court noted that "the
receipt of reformation on the Internet requires a series of affirmative steps more deliberate and directed than merely
turning a dial." The Court added that "the Internet is not as
'invasive' as radio or television."

It was the right result, but it was based on unstable
ground. In future trials, the supporters of censorship will do
everything they can to show that indecent Internet content
can spring out at unsuspecting children. . . . And as the
boundaries between the Internet and television continue to
erode, with more and more people getting wired and increasingly high-quality video programming available online, the
analogy between the media will become harder to resist. The
Court has not overruled its ill-considered holding in *Pacifica*.
It has simply found a flimsy technical excuse for not applying it to the Internet.

Nor does the potential reach of the pervasiveness doctrine
end with the Internet. Author Wendy McElroy, former president of Feminists for Free Expression, comments: "Taken to
its logical conclusion, the pervasiveness argument would prohibit anyone standing on a public street from discussing . . .
controversial matters. The open air might well transmit the
discussion through the open windows of nearby houses, businesses, and apartments. One might reply, 'Let them close the
window.'"

In *Pacifica*, the Court failed to explain why books and magazines are not pervasive. Previous generations of American
children saw their first nude image not on the Internet or
cable TV but in the pages of a *Playboy* found in Dad's closet.
As Justice Brennan pointed out, a child flipping through the
pages of the Bible is apt to stumble across a passage pertain-
ing to excrement, urination, rape, or incest. The danger of the
pervasiveness doctrine is a matter of simple logic: If the pervasiveness of a medium is an excuse for censorship, and all
media are pervasive, all media can be censored.

"Taken literally," says Washington, D.C., attorney and First Amendment specialist Robert Corn-Revere, "the pervasiveness doctrine empowers government to exert greater control over a medium of communication to the extent it is universally available and influential. By this logic, the printing press should be subject to intensive regulation, since few media are as pervasive as print. Such reasoning is antithetical to the First Amendment."

The operative metaphor for freedom of speech in the United States was formulated eight decades ago by Oliver Wendell Holmes. Dissenting from the Supreme Court's decision in *Abrams v. United States*, he wrote: "The ultimate good desired is better reached by free trade in ideas. . . . The best test of truth is the power of thought to get itself accepted in the competition of the market." In the marketplace of ideas. every medium strives to be pervasive, and so does every idea communicated in those media. The First Amendment rule book says speakers should compete to make their messages as pervasive as possible. *Pacifica* penalizes the winners.

CHAPTER FOUR

Recent and Ongoing Controversies over Free Speech and the First Amendment

The Bill of Rights

Free Speech Is Under Attack in Post-9/11 America

Detroit News

In November 2003 the *Detroit News* published the following commentary on the status of free speech in the United States. The *Detroit News* identifies two primary types of threats to free speech in America. The first are acts and pronouncements of the federal government following the September 11, 2001, terrorist attacks—actions that the authors contend impinge on the public's right to know about and dissent from government actions. The second group of threats consists of college and high school speech codes and policies that seek to eliminate from school campuses speech deemed offensive or prejudicial. Such rules have seriously eroded free speech in places where it should be protected.

Americans' guaranteed freedom to speak their minds without fear of retaliation is under attack from both the right and the left.

Colleges, courts, government agencies and the forces of political correctness are slicing off slivers of the First Amendment's promise of free speech.

The Patriot Act, with its expanded powers to snoop into the private correspondences, conversations and reading habits of ordinary Americans, has dampened public discourse and chilled political dissent.

This is an assault on the most basic of American freedoms and threatens to erode a fundamental tool for change in the United States—the ability of a committed, and often unpopular, minority to challenge the status quo.

"One of the things that has defined the (Attorney General) John Ashcroft administration is that it is unpatriotic to dissent or to object to government policy," says Kary Moss, executive director of the American Civil Liberties Union in Michigan.

"And hand in hand with that is an increased priority on secrecy in the department itself. There are two issues—the right to speech and the right to know what our government is doing. They're intertwined."

While the closing of court proceedings such as deportation hearings and terrorism trials violates due process rights of defendants, it also impinges on free speech by limiting the public's ability to monitor and respond to the legal system.

"How can we dissent, how can we preserve our right to speech if we don't know what our government is doing?" asks Moss.

But it's not only the government that is stifling speech. Those who would object to unpleasant or offensive expressions that might be viewed by some as hurtful are also reining in the ability of Americans to say what they want.

Activists have used a variety of tactics to accomplish their objectives. They have exploited exceptions to the First Amendment to silence voices counter to their ideology. And they have persuaded universities to impose drastic speech codes on students and faculty, turning institutions that were supposed to be bastions of free speech into enclaves of repressed speech.

Silencing the Campuses

Long before September 11, college speech codes, designed to create a more friendly campus environment, began eroding free speech.

And while the goal is admirable—creating study environments that are free of hostility—it has the effect of treading on the constitutional guarantees of free expression.

For example, the harassment policy of New York's Bard College forbids conduct that "causes embarrassment, discomfort, or injury to other individuals or the community."

In essence, the contrived right not to be offended is trumping the expressed right to free speech, the crown jewel of the Constitution.

Courts tossed out early campus speech codes, including one at the University of Michigan, precisely because they impinged on free speech. The codes were revived in 1994 when the U.S. Department of Education threatened to withdraw federal funding from universities if they tolerated an environment that violated the Civil Rights Act's bans on discrimination by race or sex.

That gave universities cover to restore speech limits. The Foundation for Individual Rights in Education, a Philadelphia organization that is dedicated to tracking and eradicating threats to campus speech, says speech codes are the rule rather than the exception in higher education. To protect these codes from legal challenges, campus officials often tuck them into harassment or diversity policies.

The codes have been used to keep both conservative and liberal speakers from campus podiums, cleanse student newspapers of out-of-the-mainstream opinions and disband student groups that advocate causes deemed objectionable by other students.

Each year, student newspapers nationwide report more than 20 instances of their campus publications being stolen, often by groups that disagree with the content.

Instead of being places where even the most obnoxious ideas are dissected and debated, college campuses now are cloaked in self-imposed silence.

Making Speech a Crime

Increasingly, government officials at all levels are wrongly equating speech with criminal action.

They follow zero-tolerance trends that need to be reversed for two reasons. They chill free speech. And they fail to distinguish between crime and writing or speaking about crime.

In Mount Pleasant, a high school junior criticized his school's policy on tardiness in a paper that threw in lewd references to school staff. He was suspended for "verbally assaulting" those mentioned. But a federal judge later ruled Michigan's verbal assault law unconstitutionally vague. By definition, "verbal" is speech that can claim First Amendment protection while "assault" is a physical attack that cannot claim such protection.

Even poetry is under attack.

In Blaine, Wash., a high school student penned a poem that included scenes of murder and a suicide. He gave it to his teacher to check for spelling and style errors. The teacher took it home, read it, called police and the student was expelled. As the teen-ager's attorney later said, the boy was bounced for "writing a powerful piece of literature."

In Ann Arbor, a University of Michigan sophomore was jailed without bond for writing fiction about a rape-slaying. Prosecutors charged the student, Jake Baker, for what he was thinking and writing.

Calling Baker a threat, they used a psychological analysis to say that—someday—Baker might do something akin to what he had written. That's a scenario that would be at home in George Orwell's novel "1984"—punish someone for what they might do.

The federal court threw out the Baker case. A sophomoric fantasy, no matter how sick, is also free speech and should not draw an automatic prison term.

In California, a group of authors are defending a 15-year-old San Jose boy arrested at his home and convicted of writing a violent poem. Charged with making criminal threats, he was detained for 90 days and expelled from school. Last month [October 2003], the student was supported by writers including novelist J.M. Coetzee, who won this year's [2003] Nobel Prize for literature.

After the controversy, the so-so poem was published in California newspapers with no apparent adverse effect on society. Yet the student was disciplined for making it available in his school.

Overall, speech should be given the benefit of the doubt. It's a protected right, even if found objectionable by overly sensitive or easily alarmed officials.

America doesn't work if its citizens are afraid to speak up, to challenge the status quo, to ask hard questions.

Much of what is said will inevitably cause some to cringe, others to cheer and still others to ball up their fists.

But there is far more damage in stifling speech that is deemed hurtful or unpatriotic than there is in allowing it to flow into the open, where it will either die in the light or thrive on the strength of its reason.

Free Speech Is Not Under Attack in Post-9/11 America

Gregg Easterbrook

The following selection was published in November 2001, after the United States had begun military actions against Afghanistan in response to being attacked by terrorists on September 11. Many observers feared that the ongoing war on terror might result in the loss of freedom of speech for Americans. Some pointed out that critics of the United States were being harshly denounced and in some cases losing their jobs. In the following selection, Gregg Easterbrook contends that many people decrying the diminishment of free speech misunderstand the First Amendment. Freedom of speech means that all Americans are free to air their views but should not expect to be spared from criticism and ridicule from others, he argues. Gregg Easterbrook is a senior editor with the *New Republic* magazine and a prolific writer on social and environmental topics.

In this time of semi-war, is free speech threatened when those who denounce U.S. foreign policy or sympathize with America's adversaries are themselves denounced? Rep. Cynthia McKinney (D., Ga.) complained last week [in October 2001] that she was being "attacked for speaking" because she made an overture to a Saudi prince with anti-Israeli politics. Several college instructors around the country have been assailed by editorialists and students for condemning the U.S., reactions Ruth Flowers, an official of the American Association of University Professors, told the *Washington Post* "harken back to McCarthyism."

Set aside the hypersensitivity of equating mere criticism with the darkness of McCarthyism. What's at work here is fundamental misunderstanding of the First Amendment. It guarantees a right to free speech, but hardly guarantees speech will be without cost.

Consider Robert Jensen, a professor at the University of Texas who calls the U.S. a terrorist nation, asserts that American policy in Afghanistan is a "war of lies" and that a secretive "small elite seeking to extend its power" has tricked the public into supporting apparent anti-terrorism that is actually "the culmination of a decade of U.S. aggression." Mr. Jensen is now extremely unpopular in Texas. There is a letter-writing campaign to get him fired, and he was recently criticized by the president of his own university as a "fountain of undiluted foolishness."

His backers are saying this is an attempt to suppress Mr. Jensen's free speech. In fact, Mr. Jensen continues to speak freely and often. What they really mean is that Mr. Jensen should not have to pay any price for his views. But this misunderstands the nature of the First Amendment. Mr. Jensen's right to his expression—clearly political and protected—is absolute. But there exists no right to exemption from the reaction to what is said.

What the First Amendment Is For

When the Bill of Rights was enacted, the First Amendment was construed mainly to shield speakers from imprisonment for antigovernment views. That expression could have other costs—denunciation, ostracism, loss of employment—was assumed. Many of the original patriots took enormous risks in the exercise of speech, Patrick Henry being an obvious example. William Blackstone, the English legal theorist closely read by the Framers, argued that the essence of free speech was forbidding prior restraint: Anyone should be able to say anything, but then must live with the aftermath. A citizen should possess "an undoubted right to lay what sentiments he pleases before the public," Blackstone wrote in his "Commentaries"—which James Madison consulted often while working on drafts of the First Amendment wording—but "must take the consequences" for any reaction.

The reaction to free speech, Madison thought, would be part of the mechanism by which society sifted out beliefs. Protected by Madison's amendment, the Ku Klux Klan can spew whatever repugnant drivel it wishes. Society, in turn, shuns KKK members for the repugnant people their free speech exposes them to be. No one expects the KKK to speak without a price; its price is ostracism. Why should repugnant speech on foreign policy or terrorism be any different?

And so, though Robert Jensen has the right to say what he does, his university's president has an equal right to call him a fool. When talk show host Bill Maher says the September terrorists were brave and American pilots are cowardly, his comments fully merit First Amendment protection. But the advertisers who yanked support from his show were also within their rights: That A may speak hardly means B must fund A's speech. (Mr. Maher has since retracted his comments.) Many orchestras are now refusing to perform work by the composer Karlheinz Stockhausen, who called the World Trade Center destruction "the greatest work of art ever" (the only flaw, according to him, was that the victims "hadn't agreed to it"). Mr. Stockhausen is entitled to his bizarre views; to be boycotted is the price he pays.

Similarly when the novelist Barbara Kingsolver says "the American flag stands for intimidation, censorship, violence, bigotry, sexism, homophobia and shoving the Constitution through a paper shredder," or the novelist Arundhati Roy says George W. Bush and Osama bin Laden are "interchangeable," these statements are safeguarded. But readers may fairly respond by declining to buy Ms. Kingsolver's and Ms. Roy's books, and bookstores may fairly respond by declining to stock them. That these authors have a right to their views does not mean publishers and bookstores must promote them. It is censorship if books are seized and burned; it is not censorship if books are tossed into the trash because their authors mock the liberty that made the books possible. Indeed, expressing revulsion at the sight of a Kingsolver book is itself a form of protected speech.

Dilemmas in the relationship between the freedom of speech and the cost of speech are summed up in the case of Richard Berthold, a professor at the University of New Mexico. On Sept. 11, Mr. Berthold twice told classes, "Anyone who would blow up the Pentagon would have my vote." Students have since held rallies against Mr. Berthold, and state leaders called for his dismissal.

Supreme Court Precedent

As regards speech privilege, Supreme Court precedent is firmly on Mr. Berthold's side. In a 1987 case, *Rankin v. McPherson*, the court ruled that an employee could not be fired for saying, on hearing of the 1981 assassination attempt against Ronald Reagan, "I hope they get him." This was protected expression, the court found, not a "true threat" of bodily harm. However obnoxious, Mr. Berthold's comment was clearly facetious and not meant as a threat to the lives of Pentagon employees.

But the fact that Mr. Berthold has a First Amendment right to say that he wishes the Pentagon destroyed does not mean such speech comes without cost. Students, administrators and local leaders have a First Amendment right to find his views repulsive. Taxpayers have a First Amendment right to call for his dismissal. (No one has a right to send Mr. Berthold threats, and he has received some; "true threats" are crimes that should be prosecuted.) Writers have a First Amendment right to use Mr. Berthold as an example of the ingrates who benefit from American freedom while disparaging its guardians.

Speech must be free, but cannot be without cost.

Two Veterans Disagree over Whether Flag Burning Should Be Protected Speech

Part I: Patrick H. Brady; Part II: Gary E. May

In the 1989 case of *Texas v. Johnson*, the Supreme Court by a 5-4 margin overturned the conviction of a man convicted under a state law for burning an American flag. The Court majority ruled that flag burning was an exercise of symbolic speech expressing a political point of view and was therefore protected under the First Amendment. Whether flag burning constitutes protected speech continues to be debated in the United States, with some calling for a constitutional amendment specifically authorizing laws to ban the desecration of the flag. The U.S. Senate Committee on the Judiciary held hearings on a proposed flag burning amendment in March 2004; the following selection consists of excerpts from the testimony of two American veterans regarding the proposed amendment. Part I is by Patrick H. Brady, a retired army major general and the chairman of Citizens' Flag Alliance, a coalition of organizations that supports a constitutional amendment prohibiting flag burning. Part II is taken from the testimony of Gary E. May, a Vietnam War veteran, a professor of social work at the University of Southern Indiana, and the chairman of Veterans Defending the Bill of Rights, a group that opposes any flag desecration constitutional amendment. Their clashing arguments provide an illustration of the ongoing emotional debate in the United States over free expression and the First Amendment.

Part I: Patrick H. Brady, testimony before the U.S. Senate Committee on the Judiciary, Washington, DC, March 10, 2004. Part II: Gary E. May, testimony before the U.S. Senate Committee on the Judiciary, Washington, DC, March 10, 2004.

Part I

In 1989 the Supreme Court, in response to a flag burning by a communist, amended the Constitution by inserting flag burning into the Bill of Rights. Their decision took away a fundamental right of the American people, a right we possessed since our birth as a nation, the right to protect our flag. We believe that decision was an egregious error and distorted our Constitution. We do not believe the freedom to burn the American flag is a legacy of the freedoms bestowed on us by Madison and Jefferson and Washington and the other architects of our Constitution. To distort the work of these great men unable to defend themselves, to put flag burning side by side with pornography as protected speech, is outrageous.

We believe that some elements in our society seek to amend the Constitution through the courts out of the bright light of the public square where they would surely fail. The ACLU [American Civil Liberties Union] has said they are the guardians of the Constitution and that their hope for their agenda is through the courts. We believe that our hope is in the Constitution as defined by our Founding Fathers and that we the people are the guardians of the Constitution. One judge said the Constitution is what the courts say it is! We believe the Constitution is what the Founding Fathers said it was and it cannot be amended without the will of the people. . . .

We believe that legalizing flag burning, in addition to disfiguring the Constitution, also raises values issues and questions the kind of people we have been and want to be. We believe that our laws should reflect our values. Flag burning is not a value of the American people. . . .

We believe symbols are indispensable in a democracy. They have been called the natural speech of the soul. Our gratitude for the great bounty that is America is expressed through symbols: grave stones, obelisks, walls and the greatest of all symbols, Old Glory. The word "symbol" is from the Greek meaning a half token, which when united with its other half identified the owner. It is meant to recognize something far more elaborate than itself. That something, the other half token of the flag, is the Constitution and we the people are the owners. September 11 reminded all Americans of what veterans have always known: the unifying, comforting and inspirational magic of Old Glory, its unique and indispensable value to our society. . . .

We believe our battle for our flag is a battle for our Constitution. Our concern is not those who desecrate the flag; our concern is those who desecrate our Constitution by calling flag burning "speech." If we did not act on our belief, and correct the errors of the Court, we would violate our oath and our pledge. We would be cowards not worthy of the sweat and blood and tears of those who gave us our Constitution and all we have. We could not face the greatest generation, or the silent generations; we could not face our children; we could not face ourselves. This is a sacred debt to our Founders, to America's nobility—our veterans—to our patriots and to America's future. . . .

Fact and Fiction

FICTION: Burning the American flag is protected "speech" as defined by the First Amendment to the Constitution.

FACT: Flag burning is not speech as defined by our Founding Fathers in the First Amendment, which reads: "Congress shall make no law respecting an establishment of religion, or prohibiting the free exercise thereof; or abridging the freedom of speech, or of the press; or the right of the people peaceably to assemble, and to petition the Government for a redress of grievances." James Madison, who wrote the First Amendment, condemned flag burning as a crime. Thomas Jefferson agreed with Madison and made clear in his writings that "speech" in the First Amendment meant the spoken word, not expressive conduct. To say otherwise made freedom "of the press" a redundancy. In fact, the words "expression" and "expressive conduct" are not in the Bill of Rights, and for good reason. Activist judges have added them to the Constitution in order to promote their own political agenda.

Since our birth as a nation, we the people have exercised our right to protect our flag. This right has been confirmed by every Chief Justice of the United States and Justices on five Courts in the last century who denied that flag burning was "speech." This fact is also confirmed by current constitutional experts, 70 percent of the Congress, the legislatures of all 50 states and more than three out of four Americans.

FICTION: The flag amendment would amend the Bill of Rights for the first time.

FACT: The Supreme Court amended the Bill of Rights in 1989 when they erroneously called flag burning protected speech and took away our freedom to protect our flag. And they did so without the consent of we the people, an act forbidden by the Constitution. The flag amendment is an exercise of the true ownership of we the people over our Constitution. The flag amendment restores the Bill of Rights to the meaning intended by the Founders. The flag amendment takes ownership of our flag back from the Court and returns it to the people where it belongs and where it resided since our birth as a nation. Our question to those who spout this fiction: If the Supreme Court in 1989 had voted to protect the flag, would they then have amended the Bill of Rights?

FICTION: Flag burnings are rare and not important enough to justify changing the Constitution to punish a few miscreants.

FACT: First, there have been hundreds of flag desecrations since the Supreme Court's 1989 decision. Second, the flag amendment does not change the Constitution, but restores it. In America the frequency of an evil has nothing to do with laws against that evil. Shouting "fire" in a crowded theatre or speaking of weapons in an airport are rare occurrences, but we have laws against them and we should. It is important to understand that those who would restore the right of the people to protect the flag are not concerned with punishing miscreants who desecrate it. They are not the problem. The problem is from those miscreants who desecrate the Constitution by calling flag burning "speech." We are not amending the Constitution only to protect the flag. We are doing it primarily to protect the Constitution. . . .

Enemies of the Constitution

The flag burners are not the enemies to our Constitution. It is those who call flag burning "speech," who seek to control our Constitution, who are the real enemies.

According to Webster's Dictionary, "speech" is "the act of expressing thoughts, feelings, or perceptions by articulation of words; something spoken; vocal communication, conversation."

Our courts wrongly tell us that prayer is not protected speech, but pornography is; they will not allow the Bible or the Ten Commandments in our schools. The Supreme Court prohibits any demonstration on its steps, but allows Old Glory to be burned on our streets.

Abraham Lincoln once asked how many legs would a dog have if you called his tail a leg. The answer is four. The Supreme Court counted the tail when it said burning the flag was "speech." They were wrong. Desecration of the flag is clearly conduct. However, what concerns us most is not those who defile our flag, but those who defile our Constitution by calling flag burning speech.

Part II

Good morning. I am extremely flattered and humbled by your invitation and interest in listening to my thoughts and those of other veterans about the proposed amendment to the Constitution. I gladly accepted the invitation as yet another opportunity for me to be of service to my country.

As a Vietnam veteran who lives daily with the consequences of my service to my country, and as the son of a WWII combat veteran, and the grandson of a WWI combat veteran, I can attest to the fact that not all veterans wish to exchange fought-for freedoms for protecting a tangible symbol of these freedoms. I oppose this amendment because it does not support the freedom of expression and the right to dissent.

This is among the core principles under our Constitution that my family and I served to support and defend. It would be the ultimate irony for us to have placed ourselves in harm's way and for my family to sacrifice to gain other nations' freedoms and not to protect our freedom here at home. . . .

Wounded in Vietnam

I joined the U.S. Marine Corps while still in high school in 1967. This was a time of broadening public dissent and demonstration against our involvement in Vietnam. I joined the Marines, these protests notwithstanding because I felt that it was my duty to do so. I felt duty-bound to answer President Kennedy's challenge to "ask not what your country can do for you; ask what you can do for your country". My country was asking me to serve in Vietnam, ostensibly because people there were being arbitrarily denied the freedoms we enjoy as Americans.

During my service with K Company, 3rd Battalion, 27 Marines following the Tet Offensive of 1968 in Vietnam, I sustained bilateral above the knee amputations as a result of a landmine explosion on April 12, 1968. My military awards include the Bronze Star, with combat "V", Purple Heart, with star, Vietnam Campaign, Vietnam Service, and National Defense medals. . . .

A few years back, I mentioned the anniversary of my wounding to a colleague and asked her what she was doing in 1968. Somewhat reluctantly, she said "I was protesting the war in Vietnam." I was not offended. After all, our nation was born out of political dissent. Preservation of the freedom to dissent, even if it means using revered icons of this democracy, is what helps me understand losing my legs.

The American flag stands for a long history of love and loss, of war and peace, of harmony and unrest. But it also stands for the history of a nation unsatisfied with the status quo, of a nation always in search of a greater truth, a more perfect union. Surely it does not stand for a nation where we jail those who peacefully disagree with us, regardless of the abhorrent nature of their disagreement.

The strength of our nation is found in its diversity. This strength was achieved through the exercise of our First Amendment right to freedom of expression—no matter how repugnant or offensive the expression might be. Achieving that strength has not been easy—it's been a struggle, a struggle lived by some very important men in my life and me. . . .

Dissenting Voices Must Be Heard

As offensive and painful as flag burning is to me, I still believe that those dissenting voices need to be heard. This country is unique and special because the minority, the unpopular, the dissenters and the downtrodden, also have a voice and are allowed to be heard in whatever way they choose to express themselves that does not harm others. The freedom of expression, even when it hurts, is the truest test of our dedication to the belief that we have that right.

Free expression, especially the right to dissent with the policies of the government, is one important element, if not the cornerstone of our form of government that has greatly enhanced its stability, prosperity, and strength of our country. This freedom of expression is under serious attack today. The smothering, oppressive responses to publicly expressed misgivings about our incursion into Iraq and ad hominem attacks against those who dare to express them are alarming. "Supporting our troops" does not mean suspending critical analysis and muffling public debate and discourse.

Freedom is what makes the United States of America strong and great, and freedom, including the right to dissent, is what has kept our democracy going for more than 200 years. And it is freedom that will continue to keep it strong for my children and the children of all the people like my father, late father in law, grandfather, brother, me, and others like us who served honorably and proudly for freedom.

The pride and honor we feel is not in the flag per se. It is in the principles for which it stands and the people who have defended them. My pride and admiration is in our country, its people and its fundamental principles. I am grateful for the many heroes of our country—and especially those in my family. All the sacrifices of those who went before me would be for naught, if an amendment were added to the Constitution that cut back on our First Amendment rights for the first time in the history of our great nation. . . .

An Assault on the First Amendment

I respectfully submit that this assault on First Amendment freedoms in the name of protecting anything is incorrect and unjust. This amendment would create a chilling environment for political protest. The powerful anger that is elicited at the sight of flag burning is a measure of the love and respect most of us have for the flag.

Prohibiting this powerful symbolic discourse would stifle legitimate political dissent. If it is to be truly representative of our cherished freedoms, the flag itself must be available as a vehicle to express these freedoms.

This is among the freedoms for which I fought and gave part of my body. This is a part of the legacy I want to leave for my children. This is among the freedoms my grandfather was defending in WWI. It is among the freedoms my father and late father in law defended during their combat service during WWII. It is among the freedoms that the veterans whose voices you heard through me earlier in my testimony fought to preserve and extend.

I believe that it is time for congress to pay more attention to the voices of ordinary veterans who know first hand the implications of tyranny and denied freedoms. Our service is not honored by this onerous encroachment on constitutionally guaranteed freedoms.

The Origins of the American Bill of Rights

The U.S. Constitution as it was originally created and submitted to the colonies for ratification in 1787 did not include what we now call the Bill of Rights. This omission was the cause of much controversy as Americans debated whether to accept the new Constitution and the new federal government it created. One of the main concerns voiced by opponents of the document was that it lacked a detailed listing of guarantees of certain fundamental individual rights. These critics did not succeed in preventing the Constitution's ratification, but were in large part responsible for the existence of the Bill of Rights.

In 1787 the United States consisted of thirteen former British colonies that had been loosely bound since 1781 by the Articles of Confederation. Since declaring their independence from Great Britain in 1776, the former colonies had established their own colonial governments and constitutions, eight of which had bills of rights written into them. One of the most influential was Virginia's Declaration of Rights. Drafted largely by planter and legislator George Mason in 1776, the seventeen-point document combined philosophical declarations of natural rights with specific limitations on the powers of government. It served as a model for other state constitutions.

The sources for these declarations of rights included English law traditions dating back to the 1215 Magna Carta and the 1689 English Bill of Rights—two historic documents that provided specific legal guarantees of the "true, ancient, and indubitable rights and liberties of the people" of England. Other legal sources included the colonies' original charters, which declared that colonists should have the same "privileges, franchises, and immunities" that they would if they lived in England. The ideas concerning natural rights developed by John Locke and other English philosophers were also influential. Some of these concepts of rights had been cited in the Declaration of Independence to justify the American Revolution.

Unlike the state constitutions, the Articles of Confederation, which served as the national constitution from 1781 to 1788, lacked a bill of rights. Because the national government under the Articles of Confederation had little authority by design, most people believed it posed little threat to civil liberties, rendering a bill of rights unnecessary. However, many influential leaders criticized the very weakness of the national government for creating its own problems; it did not create an effective system for conducting a coherent foreign policy, settling disputes between states, printing money, and coping with internal unrest.

It was against this backdrop that American political leaders convened in Philadelphia in May 1787 with the stated intent to amend the Articles of Confederation. Four months later the Philadelphia Convention, going beyond its original mandate, created a whole new Constitution with a stronger national government. But while the new Constitution included a few provisions protecting certain civil liberties, it did not include any language similar to Virginia's Declaration of Rights. Mason, one of the delegates in Philadelphia, refused to sign the document. He listed his objections in an essay that began:

> There is no Declaration of Rights, and the Laws of the general government being paramount to the laws and constitution of the several States, the Declaration of Rights in the separate States are no security.

Mason's essay was one of hundreds of pamphlets and other writings produced as the colonists debated whether to ratify the new Constitution (nine of the thirteen colonies had to officially ratify the Constitution for it to go into effect). The supporters of the newly drafted Constitution became known as Federalists, while the loosely organized group of opponents were called Antifederalists. Antifederalists opposed the new Constitution for several reasons. They believed the presidency would create a monarchy, Congress would not be truly representative of the people, and state governments would be endangered. However, the argument that proved most effective was that the new document lacked a bill of rights and thereby threatened Americans with the loss of cherished individual liberties. Federalists realized that to gain the support of key states such as New York and Virginia, they needed to pledge to offer amendments to the Constitution that would be added immediately after its ratification. Indeed, it was not until this promise was made that the requisite number of colonies ratified the document. Massachusetts, Virginia, South Carolina, New Hampshire, and New York all included amendment recommendations as part of their decisions to ratify.

One of the leading Federalists, James Madison of Virginia, who was elected to the first Congress to convene under the new Constitution, took the lead in drafting the promised amendments. Under the process provided for in the Constitution, amendments needed to be passed by both the Senate and House of Representatives and then ratified by three-fourths of the states. Madison sifted through the suggestions provided by the states and drew upon the Virginia Declaration of Rights and other state documents in composing twelve amendments, which he introduced to Congress in September 1789. "If they are incorporated into the constitution," he argued in a speech introducing his proposed amendments,

> Independent tribunals of justice will consider themselves in a peculiar manner the guardians of those rights; they will be an impenetrable bulwark against every assumption of power in the legislative or executive; they will be naturally led to resist every encroachment upon rights expressly stipulated for in the constitution by the declaration of rights.

After debate and some changes to Madison's original proposals, Congress approved the twelve amendments and sent them to the states for ratification. Two amendments were not ratified; the remaining ten became known as the Bill of Rights. Their ratification by the states was completed on December 15, 1791.

Supreme Court Cases Involving Freedom of Speech

1919

Abrams v. United States
Supreme Court for the first time splits in a seditious speech case involving a leaflet questioning U.S. policy in Russia; Holmes, joined by Justice Louis Brandeis, dissents from the majority's view that the "clear and present danger" test is met.

Debs v. United States
The Supreme Court upholds the conviction of Eugene Debs, arguing that his speech obstructed military recruiting and thus represents a "clear and present danger" to the United States.

Schenck v. United States
For the first time the Court reviews a free speech challenge to a federal statute (the 1917 Espionage Act). The act is upheld. Justice Oliver W. Holmes, writing for a unanimous Court, develops the "clear and present danger" test as a limit on free speech rights.

1925

Gitlow v. New York
The Court for the first time agrees that the federal free speech protections apply to the states under the Fourteenth Amendment.

1927

Whitney v. California
The Supreme Court upholds the conviction of a person charged with organizing the Communist Labor Party in California.

1931

Stromberg v. California
The Supreme Court for the first time voids a state law on free speech grounds; the case involves a California statute making it a crime to display a red (Communist) flag.

1937

Herndon v. Lowry
The Supreme Court uses the "clear and present danger" test for the first time since *Schenck* in 1919; it overturns the conviction of a Communist Party worker in Atlanta, Georgia.

1940

Thornhill v. Alabama
The Supreme Court rules that nonviolent picketing is included in freedom of speech.

1942

Chaplinsky v. New Hampshire
The Court rules that "fighting words" that cause immediate public danger are not protected by the First Amendment.

1943

West Virginia State Board of Education v. Barnette
The Court rules that the compulsory salute of the American flag by schoolchildren violates the First Amendment's free speech clause.

1949

Terminello v. Chicago
The Court reverses the conviction of a person arrested for disorderly conduct after people rioted during his public lecture, arguing that speech that potentially stirs people to anger does not meet the "clear and present danger" test.

1951

Dennis v. United States
The Court upholds the conviction of American Communists under the Smith Act, a federal law banning advocacy of the violent overthrow of the U.S. government.

Feiner v. New York
In an apparent reversal of its *Terminello* decision, the Court upholds the disorderly conduct conviction of a person who refused to stop speaking amid fears of riots despite a request by police officers; the Court rules it must balance free speech with "the interest of the community in maintaining peace and order in the streets."

1957

Roth v. United States
The Supreme Court rules that "obscene" material is not protected under the First Amendment.

Yates v. United States
Reversing itself somewhat from the *Dennis* decision, the Supreme Court overturns the convictions of fourteen members of the Communist Party in California for violating the Smith Act; the Court draws a distinction between stating an idea and advocating that a certain action be taken.

1965

Lamont v. Postmaster General
The Supreme Court for the first time voids a federal statute on free speech grounds; the overturned law had empowered the federal government to withhold delivering foreign mail judged to be "communist political propaganda."

1968

United States v. O'Brien
The Court rules that burning one's draft card as a statement of protest against the Vietnam War is not protected by the First Amendment.

1969

Brandenburg v. Ohio
The Court extends free speech rights by saying threatening speech can be protected unless the state can prove such speech is "directed to inciting or producing imminent lawless action and is likely to incite or produce such action."

Tinker v. Des Moines School District
In a case involving students wearing black armbands in symbolic protest of the Vietnam War, the Supreme Court holds that the First Amendment protects public school students' right to express political and social views.

1973

Miller v. California
The Court works out a three-part definition of obscenity as something that appeals to prurient interests, describes sexual conduct in an offensive way, and has no literary, artistic, political, or scientific value.

1976

Buckley v. Valeo
Ruling that in political campaigns "money is speech," the Supreme Court strikes down laws restricting how much an individual can spend on behalf of a candidate through independent expenditures.

1986

Bethel School District v. Fraser
The Supreme Court upholds the power of school officials to discipline a student for making a sexually suggestive (but not obscene) speech.

1989

Texas v. Johnson
The Court rules that citizens have the right to make a political statement by burning a privately owned U.S. flag.

1992

RAV v. St. Paul
The Supreme Court strikes down a city ordinance that prohibits certain symbols and that had been used to convict a white juvenile of burning a cross in a black family's yard.

1997

Reno v. American Civil Liberties Union
The Supreme Court strikes down the Communications Decency Act, which Congress had passed in an attempt to control Internet content.

2000

United States v. Playboy Entertainment Group
The Court rules that cable television content be given greater First Amendment protection than that afforded to broadcast television.

2002

Ashcroft v. Free Speech Coalition
The Supreme Court strikes down the 1996 Childhood Pornography Prevention Act, which bans "virtual" child pornography not involving actual children being filmed.

Books

Richard L. Abel, *Speaking Respect, Respecting Speech*. Chicago: University of Chicago Press, 1998.

Walter Berns, *The First Amendment and the Future of American Democracy*. Washington, DC: Regnery, 1985.

Randall P. Bezanson, *Speech Stories: How Free Can Speech Be?* New York: New York University Press, 1998.

Lee C. Bollinger and Geoffrey R. Stone, eds., *Eternally Vigilant: Free Speech in the Modern Era*. Chicago: University of Chicago Press, 2002.

Irving Brant, *The Bill of Rights: Its Origin and Meaning*. Indianapolis: Bobbs-Merrill, 1965.

Tammy Bruce, *The New Thought Police: Inside the Left's Assault on Free Speech and Free Minds*. Roseville, CA: Forum, 2001.

Archibald Cox, *Freedom of Expression*. Cambridge, MA: Harvard University Press, 1981.

Michael Kent Curtis, *Free Speech, "The People's Darling Privilege": Struggles for Freedom of Expression in American History*. Durham, NC: Duke University Press, 2000.

Richard Delgado and Jean Stefancic, *Must We Defend Nazis? Hate Speech, Pornography, and the New First Amendment*. New York: New York University Press, 1997.

Alan M. Dershowitz, *Shouting Fire: Civil Liberties in a Turbulent Age*. Boston: Little, Brown, 2002.

Richard Dooling, *Blue Streak: Swearing, Free Speech, and Sexual Harassment*. New York: Random House, 1996.

Stanley Eugene Fish, *There's No Such Thing as Free Speech, and It's a Good Thing, Too*. New York: Oxford University Press, 1997.

Owen M. Fiss, *The Irony of Free Speech*. Cambridge, MA: Harvard University Press, 1996.

Mike Godwin, *Cyber Right: Defending Free Speech in the Digital Age*. New York: Random House, 1998.

Robert Justin Goldstein, *Burning the Flag: The Great 1989–1990 American Flag Desecration Controversy*. Kent, OH: Kent State University Press, 1996.

Kent Greenawalt, *Fighting Words: Individuals, Communities, and Liberties of Speech*. Princeton, NJ: Princeton University Press, 1995.

David Hamlin, *The Nazi/Skokie Conflict: A Civil Liberties Battle*. Boston: Beacon Press, 1981.

Alan Haworth, *Free Speech*. London: Routledge, 1998.

Nat Hentoff, *The First Freedom: The Tumultuous History of Free Speech in America*. New York: Delacorte, 1980.

Steven J. Heyman, ed., *Hate Speech and the Constitution*. New York: Garland, 1996.

Mary E. Hull, *Censorship in America: A Reference Handbook*. Santa Barbara, CA: ABC-CLIO, 1999.

Peter Irons, ed., *May It Please the Court: The First Amendment: Transcripts of the Oral Arguments Made Before the Supreme Court in Sixteen Key First Amendment Cases*. New York: New Press, 1997.

Harry Kalvern Jr., *A Worthy Tradition: Freedom of Speech in America*. New York: Harper & Row, 1988.

Sheila Suess Kennedy, ed., *Free Expression in America: A Documentary History*. Westport, CT: Greenwood, 1999.

Milton Konvitz, *First Amendment Freedoms*. New York: Cornell University Press, 1963.

Alan Charles Kors, *The Shadow University: The Betrayal of Liberty on America's Campuses*. New York: Free Press, 1998.

Laura J. Lederer and Richard Delgado, eds., *The Price We Pay: The Case Against Racist Speech, Hate Propaganda, Pornography*. New York: Hill and Wang, 1995.

Leonard W. Levy, *Legacy of Suppression: Freedom of Speech and Press in Early American History*. New York: Harper & Row, 1963.

David Lowenthal, *No Liberty for License: The Forgotten Logic of the First Amendment*. Dallas: Spence, 1997.

Laurence R. Marcus, *Fighting Words: The Politics of Hateful Speech*. Westport, CT: Praeger, 1996.

Alexander Meiklejohn, *Free Speech and Its Relation to Self-Government*. New York: Harper, 1948.

Paul Murphy, *The Meaning of Freedom of Speech*. Westport, CT: Greenwood, 1972.

Russell Nye, *Fettered Freedom*. East Lansing: Michigan State University Press, 1949.

David M. Rabban, *Free Speech in Its Forgotten Years*. Cambridge, UK: Cambridge University Press, 1997.

Bernard Schwartz, *The Great Rights of Man*. New York: Oxford University Press, 1980.

Rodney A. Smolla, *Free Speech in an Open Society*. New York: Knopf, 1992.

John D. Stevens, *Shaping the First Amendment*. Beverly Hills, CA: Sage, 1982.

Nadine Strossen, *Defending Pornography: Free Speech, Sex, and the Fight for Women's Rights*. New York: Scribner, 1995.

Samuel Walker, *Hate Speech: The History of an American Controversy*. Lincoln: University of Nebraska Press, 1994.

Frank Walsh, *Sin and Censorship: The Catholic Church and the Motion Picture Industry*. New Haven, CT: Yale University Press, 1996.

Nicholas Wolfson, *Hate Speech, Sex Speech, Free Speech*. Westport, CT: Praeger, 1997.

Periodicals

Jack M. Balkin, "Digital Speech and Democratic Culture: A Theory of Freedom of Expression for the Information Society," *New York University Law Review*, April 2004.

Bradley C. Bobertz, "The Brandeis Gambit: The Making of America's First Freedom," *William and Mary Law Review*, February 1999.

Greg Costa, "John Marshall, the Sedition Act, and Free Speech in the Early Republic," *Texas Law Review*, March 1999.

Robert M. Cover, "The Left, the Right, and the First Amendment: 1918–1928," *Maryland Law Review*, Summer 1981.

Larry D. Eldridge, "Before Zenger: Truth and Seditious Speech in Colonial America, 1607–1700," *American Journal of Legal History*, July 1995.

Ivan Hare, "Inflammatory Speech: Cross-Burning and the First Amendment," *Public Law*, Autumn 2003.

Charles F. Hinkle, "Can Campaign Finance Reform Coexist with the First Amendment?" *Human Rights*, Winter 1998.

Laura Leets, "Should All Speech Be Free?" *Quill*, May 2001.

John Leo, "Campus Censors in Retreat," *U.S. News & World Report*, February 16, 2004.

Leonard W. Levy, "Freedom of Speech in Seventeenth-Century Thought," *Antioch Review*, Spring 1999.

Steven Lubet, "Picking Your Fights," *American Lawyer*, October 2003.

David M. Rabban, "The IWW Free Speech Fights and Popular Conceptions of Free Expression Before World War I," *Virginia Law Review*, August 1994.

Frederick Schauer, "The Boundaries of the First Amendment: A Preliminary Exploration of Constitutional Salience," *Harvard Law Review*, April 2004.

Alisa Solomon, "The Big Chill," *Nation*, June 2, 2003.

Geoffrey R. Stone, "Abraham Lincoln's First Amendment," *New York University Law Review*, April 2003.

———, "The Origins of the 'Bad Tendency' Test: Free Speech in Wartime," *Supreme Court Review*, 2002.

Stuart Taylor Jr., "How Campus Censors Squelch Freedom of Speech," *National Journal*, July 12, 2003.

Thomas E. Wheeler II, "Slamming in Cyberspace: The Boundaries of Student First Amendment Rights," *Computer & Internet Lawyer*, April 2004.

G. Edward White, "The First Amendment Comes of Age: The Emergence of Free Speech in Twentieth-Century America," *Michigan Law Review*, November 1996.

Web Sites

American Civil Liberties Union (ACLU), www.aclu.org/Free Speech/FreeSpeechMain.cfm. The ACLU was founded in 1920 to defend Americans' civil rights and liberties guaranteed in the Constitution. This section of their Web site focuses on free speech, including information on current cases.

Avalon Project: The American Constitution—a Documentary Record, www.yale.edu/lawweb/avalon/constpap.htm. A project of the Yale Law School, the Web site features primary source historical documents relevant to the history of the creation of the U.S. Constitution and Bill of Rights.

First Amendment Center, www.firstamendmentcenter.org. The center, affiliated with the Freedom Forum, a nonpartisan foundation, serves as a forum for the study of free expression issues. Its Web site includes information, analysis, commentary, case law, and historical articles on First Amendment topics.

First Amendment Online, http://1stam.umn.edu. A project of the University of Minnesota Law School and its professors, students, and library staff, this Web site provides publicly accessible information, ideas, and images concerning the First Amendment, including historical documents.

Morality in Media, www.moralityinmedia.org. This Web site provides information on the federal and state obscenity laws and the organization's efforts to fight obscenity in the media and the Internet.